Two Heads
in
Two Decades

Arthur Kitchin

First published by Busybird Publishing 2021

Copyright © 2021 Arthur Kitchin

ISBN
Print: 978-1-922465-71-9

Cover concept: Arthur Kitchin

Cover design: Busybird Publishing

Layout and typesetting: Busybird Publishing

busybird
publishing

Busybird Publishing
2/118 Para Road
Montmorency, Victoria
Australia 3094
www.busybird.com.au

To my mum and dad, who have struggled so much in their lives, before they got married and also after they got married.

Their love and care, for all of their six children and seven grandchildren, could not have been any better.

Warning:
My life story, in this select chapter of my life, contains: comedy, sex, controversy and is only suitable for adults.

Chapters and Abbreviations:
Brain: H.1.
Penis: H.2.
Comedy, Sex, Controversy: C.S.C.
Never Forget Moment: N.F.M.
Life Lesson: L.L.
Bullshit: B.S.
Lucky Phil: L.P.
Betrayed: B.
Bacon on Bread: B.B.
Victorian Bitters: V.Bs
Beer Battered Bunny: B.B.B.
Set Up Number One: S.U.1
Set Up Number Two Big Time: S.U.2 B.T.
Close Encounter One: C.E.1
Close Encounter Two: C.E.2
Close Encounter Three: C.E.3
Close Encounter Four: C.E.4
Olympic Village: O.V.
Camping: B.B. – V.B. – B.B.B.

Contents

Introduction

Art and Al are brothers, whose bond together is beyond words.

Brothers who grow up together in tough times experience an incredible life together. They teach each other about life, friends, relationships, family, neighbours, acquaintances, clients, and even the bad people they have had the unfortunate experience to have known.

I, Arthur, now at sixty-eight-years-old, have been very lucky in life due to the many people who I have met, who have given me good advice, taught me right from wrong, how to truly love someone, and how to know when to back off and not go any further with a friendship or relationship. I believe family is the most important component of life, followed by love within the family. The closest relationship possible between brothers is what I would like to share with you.

The five factors that have helped me through life have been:

1. Love; from family, partners, friends – thank you.
2. Happiness, laughter – it makes you feel good inside
3. Trust – a very easy word to say, but very hard to find.
4. H.1 + H.2, very helpful.
5. Words can be more dangerous than bullets or bombs. Words can also be the most exhilarating, inspiring things one person can say to another person. Words can make you cry, or laugh until you cry – I know which one I prefer.

I hope my story will help some people to secure a happy, healthy and satisfying life by using or learning something from my experiences.

I also hope my experiences will be able to make you laugh, joke, and talk about life, before bureaucracy stops us from writing, talking, expressing our inner feelings towards other people, or each other.

Chapter 1

Warrandyte to Olympic Village

At the start of my story, our family consists of Arthur (me), Allan (brother), and my two sisters (two more to follow later). We all lived in the little town outside Melbourne called Warrandyte. Dad was the local milkman, with horse and cart in the early mornings, then postman on a push bike in the afternoons.

After the Olympic Games in 1956, the government at the time released the housing built for the Olympics to the public to rent. This caught Dad's attention. He said, 'They need more milkmen in the city now.'

Mum and Dad made a very hard decision to apply for a house in the Olympic Village housing commission development. They said we children needed schooling, and neighbours, and friends to grow up with. Mum and Dad loved the country life, but Warrandyte was so small. Olympic Village in West Heidelberg had everything we needed, I can remember Dad saying, with a school and bus transport all close by.

I was just old enough to start school at five when we moved from Warrandyte. Dad was lucky enough to get a job as a milkman at the local dairy. We moved into a concrete house with three bedrooms: one for Mum and Dad, one for Al and me, and one for my two sisters (this house was twice the size of the one in Warrandyte). The house was joined onto another house by a party wall and the adjoining house was exactly the same as our house. In fact, the whole street was the same type of house, very compact and comfortable.

Life got very busy. Dad worked three jobs, I guess to pay for all our needs to survive. He worked seven days a week as a milkman, starting at 12.30 am till 6.00 am, then home for breakfast, then 8.00 till 4.00 pm as a road worker for Heidelberg Council, then on weekends he laid concrete. Lots and lots of concrete.

Chapter 2

Early Years

Mum and Dad would often say to me, 'Look after your brother and sisters, teach them what you can.'

I had no idea then that our early experiences at this time would influence our lives further down the track.

The only time we all got together was at tea time, 'family happy hour', we called it. We would all sit around the table and talk about our experiences, our friends. Mum and Dad would always make us laugh with jokes and funny things in life, and encourage us to learn from each other.

Dad loved Mum so much, he was always making her happy. Mum loved fish (live ones) so Dad built her a fish pond in the backyard, out of concrete and stones, of course. We all had a fish with a name, and it was our responsibility to look after them.

Mum also loved birds. First budgies, then canaries, then rosellas, parrots and cockies. They could talk back to you. Mum trained them to say, 'Pretty boy', 'Hello' and 'Cocky wants a cracker'. Dad also built a birdcage – started small and ended up big. Then Mum wanted chooks, 'for eggs,' she said, so up went a chook pen. We had lots of eggs from them and Mum also had a vegie garden. She was very proud of it and fed us with lots of its goodies.

Every now and then Dad would say, 'This chook is getting too old, time for dinner.' Mum would not be very happy, but knew this had to happen sooner or later. This meant off with its head, soaked in water, then plucked, cooked and served up for tea. At first no one was hungry, but after tasting the chicken (it was so good), many more followed.

Dad also had a habit of catching rabbits. When he would leave home a bit earlier to do a milk run, he would first set up rabbit nets and snare nets, then on his way home he would pick them up. Lots of rabbits. Dad always knew where the rabbits were – he could see them when delivering milk. Mum cooked them in many ways. Baked was my favourite, stewed was Dad and Al's favourite, and my sisters loved rabbit any way Mum cooked them. Mum's favourite was rabbit pie.

As all of us kids were now at school and with lots of street activity, there were always things to do and think about, from billy carts and marbles to hidey and brandy. Brandy is a game where you try to hit someone with a tennis ball. I think, the way things are today, this game no longer exists.

There was also cricket and football, played in the street, on the road, anywhere. Our street was full of other families similar to ours – lots of kids, big family, always playing different games. Some of these games have been lost over the years, unfortunately. I do not see marbles played anymore. Hidey, in the street or backyard or inside the house, all with boundaries, was such good fun – finding places to hide, in gardens, up trees, under cars (not recommended these days).

Mum had lots of work to do at home, looking after everybody, but also took on a part-time job cleaning factories or houses while we were at school.

Getting back to our happy hour at tea time, Dad would sit at the top end of the table, me on his right hand side, Al on my right hand side, and our sisters between Al and Mum. Dad would usually ask my little sisters what they did during the day. It was usually the same thing. Playing games, toys and reading were their favourites, followed by music. Mum loved playing records. Dad's favourite present for her was a new record, usually Elvis and Rock & Roll songs. And our sisters would dance with Mum all the time.

When Dad asked me one day, how did I go at school, I replied 'not very well.'

'What happened?' Dad asked.

As I was in my last year of primary school, I told Dad I liked a girl in my class and I often walked home with her on the way to our house. Her house was different to our house. It was a single house, free standing in an area with all single houses. Dad told me how he had heard of this area of houses, and the people were not so friendly like the people in our area – I found this hard to believe. Dad went on to explain it might be best not to upset the girl's family, so from now on do not walk to her house. I was very disappointed and Dad said it was for the best.

Around this time another experience occurred in our street. On Sunday morning a small car towing a small caravan would park just up the road from our house, and a young lady in a beautiful uniform would open up the caravan and then go and knock on doors in our street, asking if any children would like to visit the caravan and learn about Jesus. Mum thought this was a good idea and encouraged us to visit the caravan each Sunday morning. First Al and I would go into the caravan, and sometimes other children would be there. We were mesmerised by the stories this lady read from the Bible. Her voice was so soft at times, and so rough at other times. It was such an experience to learn about the past history in a story format, read with such passion. The Salvos Van, as it became known, grew more and more popular as other children also wanted to learn. Our sisters would sometimes go, but not like Al and me.

This went on for years. We always told Mum and Dad about the story each night at happy hour. The children were learning a lot about the Bible and the good work the Salvos do to help people even poorer than us. We did not realise how poor some people were, with not even enough food for them to eat. We always finished with a prayer for the poor people. This went on for several years, but as time went on the van stopped coming. We were disappointed, but soon we found other things to do on Sundays.

At this stage, billy cart racing was the going thing within our street. We made many different types of billy carts from anything we could get our hands on. The best to start with were milk crates (plenty of them around) on timber frames and old pram wheels. They did the job, but not very fast. This led to the best ones made from old timber packing boxes with ball bearing wheels from old truck axels (donated by Dad's work mates at the council workshop). Very fast and dangerous – hard to stop but lots of fun. Sparks would fly out of these ball bearing wheels on the asphalt roadway. At night it looked exciting – adding a hand held brake with a metal plate on the bottom to scrape on the road looked even more exciting.

Chapter 3

Second Decade. Early Year Pets – L.L.

Not long after Dad built a chook shed for Mum. I asked Dad if we could build a pigeon shed. He was happy to do this.

'Above the chook shed is the best spot for it,' he said.

So, next weekend Dad had off from concreting, up went the pigeon shed. Al, Dad and I got it up in one day, ready for pigeons.

Through my paper round, I knew a house that had a lot of pigeons. We bought four pigeons, one each – Al, my sisters and me. Different colours, different types. Each one had a name. My sisters had Snow White and Brownie, Al had Bluee, and me, Spottie, a Fantail.

We were told to keep them in the shed for two weeks to get them familiar with our backyard. We looked after them very well, spoiling them with food and handling them within the shed. After about three weeks, we thought it okay to let them out of the shed to fly free into our backyard. It all looked okay – at the start they flew around the house in circles for a while, landing on the roof. We were told to get them back into the shed, just sprinkle the food seed on the ground and into the shed. This seemed to work, but getting them into the shed part did not work.

Come late into the day, Mum said they will go in overnight. Next morning, no pigeons. All of us were very upset, so Mum said we would go and see the previous owners about one kilometre away.

Upon arrival at their house, with about fifty pigeons on their roof, I pointed out some of our pigeons. Others looked similar.

The owner's two brothers (a lot older than Al and me) told Mum that all the pigeons on the roof were theirs. 'Some might look like yours, but are not yours.'

They then offered to sell us more pigeons – Mum argued this without success, and so we left very upset about our loss.

Mum told Dad when he came home from work. Dad said he knew this family and had heard how bad they are.

Dad said he will get us some pigeons from someone else. That week he bought home four pigeons – one each and similar to our old ones, these ones had rings on their legs to identify them. This was great. We were all very happy and they stayed with us for a long time, even breeding and having baby birds. These were very interesting times, and my sisters were very excited.

Chapter 4

Lost His Marbles – L.L., N.F.M.

One of our Saturday regular sports was playing marbles on other long driveways on one side of our street.

It was a chance to show your skill and win marbles from opponents, which could then be sold onto the losers to try and get more marbles back. This was very lucrative for some players, but cheating and bullying also existed within these games. After seeing my little brother being cheated out of some of his marbles by the local bully boy – Bob and his mates – I thought I might teach him a lesson, as it was close to Guy Fawkes Night when lots of firecrackers were around.

It was a lot of fun at this time of year for us kids, with building bonfires being the main attraction and the firecrackers getting bigger and bigger each year. There were also penny bangers – three penny bangers and six penny bangers (this one more like dynamite).

I thought a penny banger set off behind bully Bob might teach him a lesson by frightening him and telling him to stop cheating on the other players. In those days, when playing marbles you would set up a target of, say, six or ten to hit at various distances apart – closer for six, further for ten. The person setting up the target to collect the shooter's marbles usually sat on the concrete driveway, legs apart, and marbles stacked as a target in front of them, very close to their groin.

The shooter rolls marbles to hit the target. If they hit it they win the marbles; if they miss, the person who owns the marbles keeps the marble. As the driveway had a slight slope falling towards the shooter, the person with the marble target would grab the rolling marble before it rolls back down the drive and keep it, which was fair enough. But sometimes this boy, Bob, would grab the marble before it looked like it was going to hit the target and keep it. Not good.

Anyway, back to the penny banger idea. To teach bully Bob a lesson, when no one else was behind him I lit up a penny banger and sat it on the path behind him about two feet away. As I walked away, I slowly looked back and, to my surprise, the penny banger was rolling towards bully Bob's backside. I could see it was too late to run back – then *bang*. Off it went.

Well, Bob jumped up, screaming, and ran home. Kids started laughing when they saw smoke and paper pieces of the firecracker smouldering on the footpath where Bob was sitting. I panicked and also ran home – this being a Saturday afternoon and me shaking so much, I knew I was in deep shit.

Dad had just got home and saw me looking a bit pale and said, 'Are you alright, son?'

'No,' I said, and told Dad what had just happened. He could not believe what I had done. Before I could fully explain the whole story, there was a knock on the front door. Sis ran to open the door and saw three people on the front porch.

'Is your dad home?' an old scruffy-looking man grunted out, and before Sis had a chance to reply, Dad, upon hearing this voice, jumped out of his chair and hurried to the front door. We all followed Dad – me, Al, Mum, and my sisters all at the front door. It was bully Bob's mum and dad. And Bob was there, crying. Bob's dad happened to be one of the bosses on the road gang at the council.

I did not know this. But I did know I was in big trouble now. Bob's dad was very angry – he was yelling at Dad, threatening to ring the police about what happened to Bob. Bob's mum was crying, standing behind Bob. I started to shake as Bob's dad told my dad that I did this deliberately to hurt Bob.

'This is not true,' I said. 'It was an accident.'

'Bullshit,' said Bob's dad. 'Bob, turn around and show them what Arthur has done to you.'

Bob turned around and slowly pulled down his pants, exposing a horrible-looking big, black, bruised buttock. It looked very painful.

Dad grabbed me by the hair, and said, 'Did you do this?'

With a slight nod of my head, and before I had a chance to explain the truth about what happened, Dad told Al to go get my belt. I started to tremble, knowing Dad only threatened to use his belt if we were ever very bad.

'Get into the kitchen,' he yelled at me as Al handed him the belt. Dad told everyone to wait there, at the front door. 'Art, come with me.'

I started to cry as he led me away into the kitchen. To my surprise he asked me why I did it. I told him Bob was nasty to Al and others, and that he stole their marbles. I was feeling better telling Dad the truth.

Dad whispered 'Start yelling "sorry Dad, sorry Bob"' as Dad started hitting the kitchen chair with his belt. I was so surprised by this; I felt a big relief come over me, in between my yelling 'sorry'.

After what seemed like five minutes – but was probably only two – Dad stopped and went over to the fridge. As he was yelling at me, 'never touch fireworks again,' he pulled out an onion. This also surprised me. He quickly cut it in half, rubbed it on his hands and then rubbed it around my eyes. My eyes instantly started to water, then they ran like a tap.

'Rub them,' he whispered as he grabbed me by the hair and took me back to the front door. Al and my sisters were all crying, Mum looked shocked, and Bob and his dad were now smirking. Bob's mum was laughing, trying to hide this with her hands over her mouth.

'Say you're sorry to Bob,' Dad yelled out. I quivered at his request, but muttered out sorry to Bob with tears flowing down my face.

Dad told Bob that I would not be able to sit down for a long time, and anything like this would never happen again. 'Arthur will be punished more,' Dad spurted out.

Dad said to Bob's dad, 'I don't think this matter needs to go any farther.' As Dad also apologised to Bob and his dad, Mum said 'Arthur has learned a lesson here and I hope there is no need to contact the police.'

Bob's dad confirmed that if anything like this happens to Bob again, they will go to the police. As they walked away from our house I could hear Bob laughing. Al and my sisters were all crying, and Mum was on the verge of tears, for me, I guess. After a couple of minutes watching Bob's family walking to their home, Dad closed the door and Dad and I burst out laughing. Mum, Al and my sisters looked stunned.

'Come on, let's all sit down and I will explain,' Dad laughed.

As we all sit around the kitchen table – Mum stunned and my sisters and Al still crying, me crying with laughter and onion – Dad started to explain.

'Bob's dad is one of my work colleagues – he is not liked much because he is a bully and I guess his son is the same. An apple does not fall far from the tree.' Dad went on to explain that he believed my version of the story and told Mum and my sisters what had happened.

Mum said it looked so real that I had been punished, and then she started to laugh. Then Al and my sisters, wiping away their tears, also started to laugh. Then we all laughed so much, tears of joy came to our eyes; this laughter, for me, turned into a stomach cramp.

Mum yelled out, 'Are you alright, Arthur?'

'I can hardly talk Mum, I've got a stomach cramp,' I spurted out. The laughter seemed never-ending.

As we all calmed down, Dad said, 'Arthur now knows, and you all know, how accidents can happen. Think about things before you do them, in case something should go wrong and hurt someone. What has just happened now is only between us, as a family, no one else is to know. Okay?'

Al and my sisters nodded to each other and Mum said she was speechless.

'That does not happen very often,' Dad spurted out, and all of us burst out laughing again.

Not long after this drama, another drama occurred. We had a hand-push rotary lawn mower – it was my job to cut the front and back lawns with it. Our next-door neighbour had a petrol-type lawn mower, and sometimes they would lend it to me to mow our lawn in a quarter of the time it took to hand-mow it.

One day our neighbour's son Paul could not start their mower. I tried to help him; we got it sorted and he mowed their lawns. I asked if we could use it to do our lawns.

'Okay,' he said.

I said, 'We won't turn it off in case we can't start it again.'

We decided to lift it over a low fence on our side of the driveway to do our front lawn. Paul lifted it by the handles and I lifted it by the front two wheels. As we lowered it down onto our lawn, the two wheels I was holding rolled back, dropping the mower onto my left knee. I felt a horrible pain and looked down at my knee; my jeans were shredded and blood was pouring down my leg.

I screamed so loud that Mum and Dad came running out of the house. Dad saw straight away what happened; Paul said it was an accident. Mum got bandages, wrapped up my leg and Dad carried me to his car, off to the hospital for repairs. Lots of stitches later, part plaster cast on my leg, then back home.

'Another lesson learned,' Dad said.

Chapter 5

Big Changes – L.L.

Now in our early teens, we were living the best times of our young lives so far. We went exploring along Darebin Creek regularly, catching lizards, frogs and tadpoles. One day, we found an old car wreck driven into the creek. Al and I, looking at this dented and smashed car in the creek half full of water, saw this big roof looking at us from the water.

'Looks like an old upturned boat,' Al spurted out. We talked about this car and thought, if we can cut the roof off will it float like a boat?

What a job, with an axe and a hacksaw, it took us all day and the next day to cut it off, but it was worth it because it did float like a boat with the both of us in it. We had great fun paddling up and down the creek. At this time of the year, blackberries were everywhere – the biggest blackberries were over hanging into the creek. We often picked and ate so many blackberries that our lips would change colour. We also picked and took home quinces – Mum would make jams from them. We also discovered there was money to be made from drink bottles floating in the creek – you could get three pence per bottle when taken back to the milk bar as a refund.

We also found golf balls in dams and rivers of various golf courses. We had great fun swimming, retrieving golf balls and selling them back to the golfers at half price of new ones. As well as our above hobbies, I also started a morning paper delivery job, starting from the Olympic newsagency to various homes and flats within the area.

One Saturday morning, I had a very bad experience as I was walking up some stairs to deliver a paper to a first-floor flat – a boy a lot older than me followed me up the stairs, but stopped about halfway up. I knocked on the first-floor door, knowing the friendly man inside would always answer the door to collect the paper and give me a tip, usually six pence (tips were the added bonus to my pay for delivering papers). Not many people gave me tips for delivery; sometimes I just left the paper at their front door.

As I started to walk down the stairs, the boy, halfway down, waiting for me, said, 'I need six pence from you.'

'Why?' I said.

He then went on to say I might have a fall on these stairs and I might break an arm or leg.

I said, 'No way.' He put his arms across the stairs, blocking my path down. I felt threatened by him, so I pulled out six pence from my pocket and gave it to him.

He smiled and said, 'See you later.'

I felt very sad and upset by this. I thought I could not tell anyone about it, especially Dad or Al.

The following Saturday, as I ran up the stairs, I heard his lower-floor door close shut. I was thinking, is that him coming out? And it was. He was standing at the bottom, waiting and watching me put the tip into my pocket. As I turned to go down the stairs, he started walking up the stairs – me thinking, not again, but his demand was the same.

I said, 'This is wrong, not fair.'

'Stiff shit,' he said, again with his arms across the stairs.

I told him 'I will tell the newsagent man about you,' and he said, 'Do that and you *will* break an arm or leg falling down these stairs.'

I quickly gave him another six pence and pushed past him and ran to my next delivery. I was feeling very confused, upset. How can I stop this? Who can I talk to?

Lucky for me, a son of one of my customers, John, would always be waiting for me on his front porch. Sometimes when it was raining we would have a quick chat. He was a bit older than me. He went to Heidelberg Tech School; I went to Macleod Tech School. He was also a lot bigger in size to me. He asked me about getting a job, like me delivering papers. I told him to go see my boss at the O.V Newsagency. I told him he is a very good man, a husband and wife business, and a very kind man also.

He asked me questions about my job, do I like it, how much pay do I get? Too many questions, I thought. Then he asked me about tips, as sometimes his dad would say, 'Give Arthur a tip,' usually a threepence. I told him this was the next best part of my job – in a week I could get the same money in tips as my pay.

He then asked about any bad sides to my work. I said the worst part was the weather, rain, hail and sometimes it was very cold in the mornings. I also told him about the boy just down the road, a couple of blocks away, who was taking the tip money I got from the man living above him. John asked why, I told him this boy said I might have an accident on the stairs, might break an arm or leg, unless I gave him the money.

John was fascinated by this and asked me his name and where he lived.

'I don't know his name, he lives under the stairs in one of those two-storey flats about two blocks away.'

John said he would like to meet this boy.

I said, 'Why?'

John said, 'I don't like what he's doing to you.'

'Neither do I,' I spurted out.

He then said, 'I'll come with you next Saturday and see what happens.'

'Okay,' I said, thinking this might help me.

I could not wait to see if John was on his porch on Saturday morning. He was, thank God, I thought as I handed him the paper.

'I'll give this to Dad,' he said. 'Back in a minute.'

As we walked along my delivery round, putting papers into boxes or onto front porches, we got closer to the flats. John, always talking, non-stop, asked me about my weekends. I told him about other ways Al and I made some more pocket money: golf balls, drink bottles, scrap metal now and then. He was fascinated by this.

When we arrived at the flats I could see the boy at his window, under the stairs, and told John he was there. John said he will keep walking, then come back.

When I walked up the stairs, I heard the door under the stairs close. I knew what was next. As I turned to come down the stairs, the boy was waiting. I just stood at the top, shaking all over, not knowing what to do.

'Well,' said the boy, 'where is it?'

I said softly, 'I'm not paying you anymore.'

'What?' he yelled out.

As he started running up the stairs, my heart was racing. *I'm a goner*, I thought. Just then John appeared at the bottom of the stairs, behind the boy. I sigh with relief as John yelled out, 'Hey you!'

As the boy turned around, John straight away recognised him. John later told me they went to the same school, Heidelberg Tech. He was in the year below John.

'Steve!' John yelled. 'What's going on here?'

Steve now very slowly walked down the stairs to talk to John, and I followed him down.

'My friend Arthur tells me you think he might have an "accident" here on these steps.'

As Steve started to talk, John yelled at him, 'If you go near Arthur again, you will be the one having an "accident". Maybe a broken arm or leg. Do you understand me?'

Steve's dad heard this commotion and came out of his flat. *Shit*, I thought, we're in trouble here. Steve's dad was in shorts and covered in tattoos.

'What's the yelling about?' he said.

Steve told his dad, 'This is John from school and Arthur, his mate. They stopped by from school – everything is okay.'

His dad went back inside. John now told Steve everything better be okay from now on. As we both walked away, Steve went back inside. As we were walking, John tells me Steve was a bit of a troublemaker at school and has had run-ins with him in the past.

As we continued walking for a couple more blocks, John said, 'I don't think Steve will trouble you again.'

He was right, I never saw Steve again. Such a relief. John and I became friends. Not long after this experience, my boss asked me if I would like to sell Heralds (afternoon papers) after school at the bus stop up the road. This sounded like a good idea (no early mornings). I asked the boss if John could do my morning round. He was very happy to meet John, who got my morning round. He was very happy. Happy all round, I thought.

When I started my new job, selling the Herald at the last bus stop at O.V. from the city, it felt exciting to greet people as they got off the bus – lots of people. This bus would turn around, opposite my old school, O.V. Primary, and go back to the city to collect another load of people. This bus stop was only a couple of minutes' walk to the newsagents but people started buying from me instead of going to the shop. I started selling about twenty a day, some with tips. This quickly grew more and more – I would sell out sometimes. I used my billy cart to take bundles of papers to the bus stop because lots of people got off the bus and would go in different directions to their homes. I would be yelling out about the front line story in the paper, along with 'read all about it' and people would buy one to read about it at home.

It got to a stage where I asked Al to help me, as he wanted a cut in tips also. I noticed more and more people would give me a tip, or say keep the change upon buying the paper. This tipping grew to a point where I got more in tips than from being paid for selling the papers.

At this time I was putting my weekly paper money earnings into the state savings bank, where Mum and Dad opened a bank book account for us all when we were children and told us to save for a rainy day, encouraging us to save our pocket money.

'Put it into your bank book,' Mum always said.

This added up very quickly over the years for me, from shillings to pounds to lots of pounds. I didn't think about it that much; maybe one day I'd have enough to buy a car. That was my aim.

Al was also excited to be with me, he was always laughing and talking to people. I think he has got the gift of the gab.

All of sudden our lives were about to change. At our family happy hour, Mum and Dad told us all we were going to have another brother or sister. We were all so excited – the time went so fast, and when we saw our new sister, Gaylene, we all wanted to nurse her and spoil her. Then within another two years, Mum had another baby, Jillian. Mum said Gay needed a playmate to grow up with (the rest of us were too 'old'). Mum loved babies, even other people's babies.

Chapter 6

Bungalow – N.F.M., C.E. 1

When two more sisters arrived into our family, Mum and Dad found it very difficult to fit eight into our house. An answer to this problem was we needed a bungalow for us boys. I can remember Dad saying he could just scrape enough money for a deposit on a bungalow. I told Dad I can help pay it off with my paper round money, he laughed and said we will see. I know this was a harder time for Dad, always working. Any spare time spent with us kids, taking us on day trips to parks or visiting relatives.

The bungalow was soon put up in the backyard near the house, and it turned out to be the best thing that could have happened to us boys – our own room separate from the noise of crying babies and annoying music from our sisters. Al and I liked the more modern music, the girls were still hooked on old music that Mum liked. We felt independent and free, but this also caused problems, with limited space – only a 3.5 x 2.5 metre room to spare.

We started with a bunk bed – Al on the bottom and me on top. This set up did not last very long due to our differences and temperaments, constantly annoying one another. Al found it amusing to lift me up with his legs from below. Dad came up with another good idea: get another bunk bed so we could have our own bed each, top or bottom, plus the advantage of storage above or below each bed. This worked a treat. We also got a set of drawers each and a wardrobe to share. As we were both growing up, we needed space for our own possessions, and this created more problems. After a lot of discussion between us, I thought we could get more drawers and a larger wardrobe with drawers stacked on drawers – now a big wardrobe in a small room, not much floor space left to define our own space within the room. After much argument over drawers and the wardrobe areas, we decided to place tape on the timber floor and up the walls to give us approximately half each. This solved our problem. Hanging posters of chicks and our favourite items on walls soon filled the bungalow to breaking point.

Now at 15 and 17 years old, being together in the bungalow, Al and I started to get even closer. As I was now working, our happy hour around the tea table was not always possible for me. Sometimes Dad would pick me up from work, but he could only wait until 5.00pm at Templestowe, meaning if I had to work back to finish jobs and was not at the pick-up point (Denis's house), then I would have to make my own way home. Sometimes I would take my push bike if I knew I would be working back or doing overtime on bigger jobs. At work I would walk home – a long way from Templestowe to O.V. – and if I was clean enough (not very often after a full day of labour), I would hitch hike. Mum and Dad told me never do this but sometimes I did; I was so stuffed some days, I just did not have the energy to walk home.

Due to the time changes, with me now working and not always at the family happy hour, which made more room at the table for the rest of the family, Al and I could talk about the daily activities and he could fill me in on the happy hour that I missed. As time went on Al and I became closer about our 'personal experiences' and due to the seclusion of our bungalow from the rest of the house, we could talk about anything without our sisters asking questions all the time.

One day, not long after my 16th birthday, I called into one of my mates houses, as I often did, to ask him to go out down to the creek and hang out together. When I knocked on the door his mum answered.

'Is Tom home?' I asked.

'No,' said his mum, detailing that he had gone to the shops to buy supplies. 'Come in,' she said, 'I will make you a cup of tea or coffee.'

'Coffee sounds good,' was my reply.

'Tom might be a while,' she said.

Tom's mum started talking about her hubby while making the coffee. She said he did shift work and did not get home until the early hours in the morning. She added that Tom had a big list of things to pick up, as she sat down beside me at the table and handed me the coffee. She said to me, 'Would you like to fuck me?'

I spilt my coffee straight away, started to shake, not knowing what to say or do. She saw my reaction and said we can go to bed, no one is home.

I started to feel red in the face and frightened, not knowing what to do, just that I needed to get out of there now, as I stood up and ran out. This still haunts me today, never having told anybody what happened – except Al that night, but he would not believe me. I never went back into Tom's house – Tom and I were friends for a long time but I was scared to tell him what happened.

To add to our experiences at this time, my mates and I would sneak into the drive-in picture theatre, opposite Northland Shopping Centre, now gone. We found a spot to crawl under the wire fence adjoining the park, next to the drive-in, and watch the movies. Sometimes we were able to watch the movies, other times not. We were always watching the cars inside the carpark, looking for ones that were moving around a lot, meaning something was going on in that car or van. They were usually near us at the back of the carpark. We would laugh and joke about what was going on in that car or van; sometimes it was more interesting than the movie, as we could see the silhouettes inside from the back looking towards the big screen.

Chapter 7

End of School

With me hating school and not doing very well in most subjects: English, sporting and others, I did like maths and technical workshop – making things in metal and wood. I asked Mum and Dad if I could leave school and get a job. They said do another year (5th year) at school. I said I could not do another year, as I only just scraped through this year; enough to get me an apprenticeship. Dad said, 'Okay, get into the building industry. Everybody needs a house,' was his response.

Mum said, 'Go further, try harder at school.'

I knew which one I wanted, and told Mum I could not go back to school.

After much debate, Dad said, 'We should start looking for a job. Easier said than done.'

Eventually Dad found me a job, just after Christmas, working in a plumbing shop in Heidelberg – not too far from home. He knew the owner of the shop; it was one of his customers on the milk round. I was so excited to work. I wanted to learn everything about the shop. (Al got my paper selling job.) I started serving at the counter, running around loading up plumber's cars and trailers with hundreds of items, meeting new people, experiencing new friends, and making relationships with the owners, family businesses and customers. It was a marvellous experience, and every day I could not get to work quick enough. Now I was earning a lot more than selling papers and enjoying every day.

One day the boss asked me to do some office work, invoicing and filing, and it sounded okay. It started with a couple of hours a day when it was a bit quiet in the shop. Then it went to half a day in the shop and half a day in the office. The office was very small, full of books, and on the desk were calculators, pencils and lots of invoices. All the invoices with prices of all the items to be manually worked out, discounts calculated, from pricing books and calculator. I did enjoy maths at school; it was one of my favourite subjects.

The boss noticed I was good and quick at this job and offered to send me to a college to improve my skills and do a business course. Sounded okay, but I could not sit in a small office, day in day out, surrounded by paper, books and invoices. I wanted to be outside – fresh air, variety in work. As I got to know a lot of plumbers, I started asking them if they wanted an apprentice. (It was very hard in those days to get an apprenticeship.) It looked like a good trade, and I did now know a bit about plumbing from the supply side. Unfortunately my boss was told of my enquiries into an apprenticeship, and, as he had other plans for me, he was not a happy chappy. He told me I had one week to decide which way to go. I did not want to go to college and work inside an office all my life.

It was an easy decision to make – I wanted to work outside. I asked every plumber I could about an apprenticeship, without the boss watching me like a hawk. My luck again – on the last day, in the morning, I told my boss I was leaving. He was not very happy. He tried to talk me into staying, offering me more in wages also. That afternoon a father and son called in to collect materials as I was walking, out for a break. We bumped into one another.

'Gidday,' I said to Denis, the son, as his dad, Norm, went into the shop.

I told Denis this was my last day here. He was surprised. I told him I wanted to be a plumber like him, but could not get an apprenticeship. To my surprise he said he would talk to his dad. I gave Denis my home phone number and went back into the office. That Friday night Denis rang me and said they would give me a go, can I start next Monday?

'One hundred percent,' I said. I could not believe my luck.

Chapter 8

My Next Family – N.F.M., L.L.

The next best part of my life was meeting my new family – the Williams family. Dad (Norm), Mum (Linda), Son (Denis) and his wife Rosemary and their children.

This family-run business, Templestowe Plumbing, is still going strong today – still with Denis, and his sons and daughters. This family business was always busy, and we all worked very hard – lots of variety, lots of experiences, and lots of love within this family. They took me in as part of their family; again, I was so lucky.

The next four and a half years were the most rewarding, loving, caring and happiest experiences ever. Not only did they take me on as an apprentice plumber, but also like a family member. It was a father and son business when I joined them, working from Norm's shed and house – always busy. Working outside in all areas of plumbing, drainage, new houses, even on the many orchards in the beautiful area of Templestowe, Doncaster, and my old town, Warrandyte.

Due to the distance from Templestowe to O.V., sometimes, when we worked till very late in the day, I would stay and sleep over with Denis' family overnight, and share in their family's life. It was like a second home for me; not as crowded as my home. Denis became like a big brother to me, about ten years' difference between us. We shared everything in common that led us to buying a dirt bike each. Denis bought his 90' Suzuki dirt bike up front; I paid my same 90' dirt bike off over one year. We each had such great fun on these bikes

– in the summertime after work and on weekends.

In the mountains there was fresh air racing over my face in varying temperatures as we rode through the mountains. I enjoyed the smells, wild animals, and meeting new people who were doing the same. It was never ending fun. My bike was usually kept at Denis' house, but sometimes Dad would put it in his trailer and bring it home. At home with the bike I would let Al ride it now and then; he always wanted more time on the bike. I was concerned he would crash it and hurt himself, but we managed okay. One Christmas holiday, I brought the bike home to share with Al and my sisters. We had a ball taking it in turns riding along the creek area. I left the bike chained up in the shed; I was always worried it would get stolen when at our house – lots of things got stolen in our area.

Being Christmas holiday time, Denis and his family often went water skiing at Bonnie Doon, staying at a caravan park for starters. He invited me and some mates to come up and go skiing with them. Denis loved boats, cars and water sports, and so did I. We stayed for about a week, learning how to water ski, wake board, and tube, towed behind the boat. Again, absolutely amazing fun.

Denis loved Bonnie Doon so much that he ended up buying a holiday house there, and every year I would go up there and camp in his backyard. That first week at Bonnie Doon, when I left the bike at O.V., the temptation for Al to ride it was too much. I told Al where the keys to bike and chain were – what a big mistake on my part. With Al wanting to ride the bike and the sisters pressing him to take them for rides, it got too much. Al agreed to this. Al's experience with bikes was not very much, only short rides on the back with me.

First ride out, without our sisters on the back, Al soon crashed it and broke his leg. It was very bad – his leg was 90 degrees to the rest of his body. Boy, was he in trouble. But when I came home from Bonnie Doon, Mum lashed out at me for encouraging Al to ride the bike, saying it was all my fault.

Al was now in plaster on crutches for a long time.

'It's not my fault,' I said to Mum, but she blamed me for buying the bike. I did feel very sorry for Al.

I tried to tell Mum and Dad that I was always falling off the bike and sometimes had a crash, but no serious injury had happened to me.

'Lucky you,' Mum spurted out.

Trying to make a light joke about this, I told Mum that sometimes when riding the bikes I would be nominated 'best man on ground' (not the same as in football), and bike riding one weekend they even considered giving me a trophy for best man on ground.

I was now approaching seventeen and a half years old. Denis started teaching me to drive, so I could get my driver's licence. We started in Norm's old Wolseley Sedan, his pride and joy. Denis loved cars – he had a Mini Cooper and a four wheel drive for work. At this time it was not suitable for me to learn in, he said. Norm's car was the best one to learn in, he said. I soon found out why. Denis would take me out to the back roads of Templestowe and show me what to do. Not what I expected. He loved to drive and was involved in hill climb racing with his Mini Coopers, showing me how to drift around corners, do donuts – sometimes this was helped by a beer or two.

One night sticks in my mind. At the end of a long hard Friday's work Denis said, 'After tea I'll give you another driving lesson.' He just loved driving his Dad's Wolseley. Heading off for my lesson we stopped and picked up a six-pack of beer – to quench our thirst, of course. As the daylight quickly turned to night and the cans were empty, it was time to go back to Norm's to drop off the Wolseley. In those days not many cars were on the road, especially on the back roads of Templestowe. In usual style, as we came around a bend, the Wolseley started to slide sideways. Next thing we know it's stuck on the side of the road. Denis was revving the engine, with nothing happening.

'We're bogged,' said Denis. Denis turned off the motor and lights. In pitch black I opened my passenger's side door. As I stepped out I let out a hell of a scream.

'What the—' Denis yelled out. 'Are you okay?'

I gave no answer but moaned a lot.

'Art, where are you?'

As I looked up I could see Denis' silhouette in the moonlight. He was high above me on the roadside; I was at the bottom of an embankment on my back, sore all over.

'Down here,' I yelled out to Denis.

'Are you okay?' Denis yelled out again.

'A bit sore,' I said.

'I'll come down,' said Denis. He slipped and fell down the embankment also. It was very steep. He landed next to me.

'Are you okay?' I said.

'I don't think anything is broken,' he said.

'Same here,' I said. We sat there in the dark looking up at the Wolseley sitting bottomed out on the edge of the embankment.

'Looks like we are in deep shit,' he spurted out.

We could not climb back up at this point. We had to walk about twenty metres from the car to climb back up to the road. As we walked back to the Wolseley, Denis said how lucky we were not to have rolled the Wolseley down the embankment, but how could we get it back on the road?

After considering all our options, Denis decided we should walk home to his house about two miles away, then come back in the morning to get the car using his four wheel drive. As it was now about eleven PM, when we got home Rosemary was very worried about us and gave Denis the biggest serve of language. I had never seen her so angry. Boy, were we in trouble the next day.

About seven AM Norm was knocking on the door, not a man to be angry but he was very upset. He has just been informed by the local police his Wolseley was stuck on the side of the road with lots of empty beer cans on the back seat and floor. Norm knew straight away what had probably happened. He told the police it must have been stolen from his driveway. This was accepted by the police but they had a feeling Denis was involved. Norm said he would take care of it. The police told him to remove it ASAP. Norm told Denis to go and get the Wolseley 'now', bring it back and 'never' touch it again.

With Denis's four wheel drive, we arrived to see how bad it was stuck and how lucky we were. It was in a very bad situation. Denis said we needed two cars to safely pull the Wolseley back onto the road. If we tried it might roll over the edge. Denis rang one of his mates who had a tow-truck.

'Happy to help out,' was his reply.

As we stood there, looking at the sad-looking Wolseley, grass up to the door, handles balancing on the ground, body of the car stuck at a centre point on the embankment, Denis said, 'I hope we can save it otherwise I'm in real, real trouble.'

With two slings attached to the Wolseley, one at the front, one at the back, short ones, Denis's idea was to slowly pull it back onto the road. With me in his four wheel drive at the back, his mate's tow-truck pulling from the front, Denis in the Wolseley. I did not like this idea. Denis said it was the only way to do it. When Denis' mate arrived he could not believe what he saw. Denis explained his theory to remove it back onto the road.

'Sounds okay to me,' he said. As the tow truck pulled it forward my job was to keep the tension on the back swing to stop it going down the embankment. This to me was frightening. I thought of Norm's love of this car and the possibility of it rolling down the embankment. As Denis's mate very slowly pulled it forward, Denis with the steering wheel on full lock to get it back on the road, me keeping the tension on my sling, I could see it working. The Wolseley slowly became level on the side of the road. What a relief this was. Upon inspection of the underside of the car Denis said it looked okay.

'These cars were built like a tank,' he spurted out and started laughing about the situation. Such a relief.

Not long after this Denis bought a brand new Ford GT V8. British racing green. Straight out of Bathurst type. Said he had to have one. This car was unbelievable. I had never known the power of a V8 motor, couldn't have until Denis got this car. I was hooked on V8 from this time on. I will get one, one day, I promised myself. I could not believe this Ford V8 would be the next car I would learn to drive in. It felt ten times more powerful than the Wolseley.

The next thing I will never forget is Denis said to Rosemary, 'Do you mind if Art and I go for a trip to Canberra next weekend?'

Denis said he would like to show me around the country up there. They had been there before.

'Okay, but be back before Sunday night.'

I stayed that Friday night. We took off very early Saturday morning, no traffic on the roads. Let's see what this car can do. As we flew up the highway, I didn't think anybody would have travelled the road as fast as we did. When we arrived in Canberra it was about mid-afternoon. To say it was 'dead' was an understatement. Denis showed me the usual tourist spots.

Then Denis said, 'Let's do Bathurst.' I knew this was his main aim for our trip, to take the Ford V8 for a spin around Bathurst.

When we arrived it was close to sunset. Not deterred by this, Denis said he would be able to see the headlights of any oncoming cars. Well, what a drive this was. We sat at the bottom of the truck looking up to the top of the hill.

No cars around, Denis spurted, 'Let's go!'

With wheels spinning, smoke coming from them, it seemed we were in race mode. It was incredible. Scary at times, especially at the top of the hill and down the straight.

'Got to do it again,' he yelled.

'Wow,' I yelled.

After this second lap Denis was very excited. He said, 'I want to show you another beautiful place Rosemary and I once visited – Batemans Bay.'

So off we went. After staying a night at Goulburn only to sleep, we were up early next morning.

'In for a great day today,' Denis spurted out. The sun came up as we drove towards Batemans Bay – it was a great feeling to me to be again so lucky to be exploring all this. Batemans Bay and along the coast was incredible for me. Taking in all the beautiful scenery, Denis pointed out everything he and Rosemary had seen on their trip.

As the day closed in, I said, 'Will we head back to your house tonight?'

'For sure,' said Denis. I noticed he put his foot down to go further.

As night approached I again asked, 'What time do you think we will get home?'

He said, 'Sunday night as I promised Rosemary.' We just made it before midnight, Rosemary was not very happy again.

'I was so worried about you two,' she said, knowing how Denis drove, but was also so relieved to see us both and gave us a big hug. This hug melted my heart. I had a secret crush on Rosemary (now passed away, one of the saddest days of my life). She was what I called 'drop-dead gorgeous' and a very loving mother, wife and friend. I often thought, I hope one day I can meet a girl like Rosemary.

Denis and I were so close that I started doing some invoices for the business (similar to my first job at Plumbing Supply). This gave Denis more time for his family, with me learning more, saving heaps of money due to the extra income from invoices. I soon had enough saved to buy a new car. Must be a V8. I like Holdens better than Fords. Denis was not impressed.

'I like the look of Holdens better,' I told Denis.

Chapter 9

Marilyn the Mermaid – N.F.M., C.E. 2

As teenagers, Al and I, in the summertime, loved going to the Yarra River, usually at Warringal Park, Heidelberg. Also a great place to go grass surfing. We would jump off a cliff on a bend in the river. A long way from the top of the cliff to the water, but it was very exciting showing off to the many other girls and families also swimming and enjoying themselves.

We also loved going to the Ivanhoe Public Swimming Pool. We would ride our bikes or catch the bus depending on the time and weather. Year after year, same thing. I was about seventeen-years-old, with my mates mucking around on diving boards, doing bombs, somersaults and swimming under the water from one side of the pool to the other in one breath (not so easy).

One of the days I will never forget was when, while in the pool, a young beautiful girl appeared next to me in the deep end with one hand holding on to the side of the pool and treading water to stay afloat.

She said, 'Hello.' She was a stunner, I thought she looked like a mermaid. Her eyes seemed to sparkle as she spoke about how much she loved to swim. She seemed a little bit older than me and spoke in a posh sort of voice. We talked for a while until my mates came over when they spotted me talking to her.

One of my mates at this time was named Bernie. He had the, what I called the 'gift of the gab' when it came to girls. He was able to crack jokes, make them laugh and be entertaining.

As the three mates sat on the side of the pool next to us, Bernie straight up asked, 'What's your name good looking?'

'Marilyn,' she said.

'As in Monroe?' was Bernie's instant response. 'I can see the resemblance,' he also spurted out.

I noticed Marilyn blush. She didn't even know my name yet so I said, 'I'm Arthur, and this is Bernie, Ray and Lionel.'

Straight away Bernie asked, 'Are you with friends?'

'No, I am by myself. It's too hot at home,' she explained.

'Lucky us,' Bernie spurted out again. Now Bernie seemed to be looking down at her cleavage. I was also noticing how amazing she looked. Marilyn then said to Bernie, 'I would like Arthur to show me how to swim from one side to the other side under water.'

This was something I was doing before Marilyn showed up. I felt relieved by this request as Bernie was about to jump into the pool with us. I knew that this would be the end of my conversation with Marilyn.

'Arthur show me how to do it now.' As if she knew Bernie was about to jump in. 'Show me how.'

'Well, first of all you need to hold your breath for a long time. Take a deep breath first,' I said. As she did this my eyes almost popped out of my head as she drew in a large breath. Her breasts nearly popped out of her bikini. All the boys just stared.

'That's fantastic,' I spurted out. 'Do it again.'

Big breath. Again, it made our day, I thought. I then explained how to duck under the water and push off from the side of the pool and swim front style under the water, moving arms sideways with fingers closed for extra force going forwards, and kicking less with legs. The boys could see me explaining this and decided the best show for them was over. Off they went. As we did this together for the first time I looked back at her underwater. With her eyes open, my eyes looking at her, she looked even more like a mermaid I thought. She stopped about half way and I came back to her. I asked if she was okay. She said, 'That was fantastic.'

I said, 'It takes practice to go all the way.'

Marilyn then said, 'I can go all the way.' She said this in an unusual tone of voice as if meaning something else. I did not realise then what she may have meant by this comment. As we tried several times to complete the crossing underwater we seemed to get on really well. Marilyn said she needed a rest and that her towel was on the hill, away from the pool, not far from mine as it turned out. I said I needed a rest too and, as we both got out of the pool, I noticed how drop-dead gorgeous she was. Her body glittered in the sun as she emerged from the water to reveal a perfectly proportioned female figure, again reminding me of a mermaid. Luckily Bernie and his mates didn't see us get out of the pool, so we were by ourselves on the grassy hill overlooking the pool, sunbaking on our towels amongst hundreds of other sunbathers.

'This feels great,' she said and started to tell me she lives not too far away and goes to a school close by, one of those girls-only schools. She seemed very smart and wanted to be a doctor as she was fascinated by the human body. I spurted out that I was fascinated by her body – as if this was what Bernie would say, but it was true. Marilyn laughed and said, 'I am fascinated by your body.'

I laughed.

'Why?' I asked her.

She said, 'I love a thin built, strong looking and tanned man. Not too muscular.'

'You must be talking about Bernie,' I said.

She laughed again louder and said, 'I like your body.'

To respond, I told her I liked hers too.

'Let's go for a swim,' she suggested. 'Great, underwater okay?'

'Sure,' was my reply. Marilyn suggested we hold hands and our breath for as long as we could together on the bottom of the deep end of the pool.

'Sounds great,' I said as we jumped into the pool straight to the bottom in the deep end. As soon as we hit the bottom I felt her hand go into my bathers. As she grabbed my penis, I was shocked. But her hand felt so warm on my cold penis. It started to grow instantly. She could see the look on my face – it was of shock or surprise. As we started to float to the surface I thought, how lucky am I?

When we surfaced she removed her hand and said, 'Did you like that?'

'It was unbelievable,' I spurted out. 'Thank you,' I said. It was all I could think to say.

'This is what I find fascinating about the human body,' she explained.

'How does this happen?' I asked. She just smiled. As we hung onto the side of the pool, still in the water she put her hand inside my bathers again.

'It's much bigger now. How does it feel?' she asks.

'The most exhilarating feeling I have ever felt,' I spurted out. As my penis was about to pop out of the top of my bathers she said we'd have to stay in the water for a while until it 'goes down'.

'I don't think it will ever go down.'

'It will,' she assured me. We went on talking whilst still in the water.

'What just happened?' I said. Marilyn seemed to know all about male reactions. 'Is it because you want to be a doctor?' I asked.

'Of course,' she said. I then asked her if I could touch her to feel what it's like for me and she said okay.

'Let's take a deep breath and dive underwater together again holding hands.' As we did this my heart was racing so much. I had never done this before. What was I in for? So many thoughts were racing through my head. When we touched the bottom of the pool Marilyn put my hand inside her bathers and moved it up and down over her vagina. It was so soft. Softer than anything I have ever touched, another feeling I will never forget. I wanted to stay there forever. My heart was beating so fast I had to go and rush to the surface for breath. I just made it, gasping for air. Marilyn asked if I was okay.

'That's incredible. I can't explain my feelings, how soft and smooth you are. If that's why you want to be a doctor, I want to be a doctor too.'

She laughed out loud. 'See why I think the human body is fascinating?'

As the day neared closing time for the pool I asked if I could see her again.

'Usually on a Saturday, when it is hot I will be here. I cannot come on a Sunday as it is our family day.' She laughed. 'Let's keep today to ourselves. Don't tell anyone about it.'

'That's a deal for sure. I do not want Bernie or my mates to spoil this.'

'Great,' she said.

'See ya maybe next week.'

As I watched her walk out of the pool centre I noticed she waited at the bus stop to catch the next bus and within minutes she was gone. When this happened I thought I should have asked for her phone number or address and a lot more about her. Too late now.

The following Saturday I could not get to the pool quick enough. Although it was not a very hot day, I laid on the same grassy hill watching the bus stop for hours. My mates thought I was sick just lying there watching. As the day wore on I felt I would not see Marilyn again. When we left the pool I felt I had lost someone special in my life. For many weeks I kept going to the pool on Saturdays. No Marilyn.

Then one very hot Sunday afternoon when we went to the pool I spotted Marilyn on the grassy hill. My heart started racing again. There were hundreds of people everywhere but she stood out, just sitting on her towel, talking to a man. As I started walking towards her, the man she was talking to walked away. You beauty, I thought as I started running towards her. I could she her roll over on her towel to sunbake her back. As I arrived next to her there was just enough room for me to sit next to her.

'Good afternoon Marilyn,' I said and she slowly rolled onto her side. She looked even more beautiful than when I saw her last time, I thought.

'Arthur,' she said.

'Long time no see,' I said. I told her I have been trying to see her again for weeks. Marilyn explained how she had been very busy studying all week and not going out much.

I said, 'I need your phone number so I can ring you in the future.'

Straight away Marilyn told me she now has a boyfriend – I just missed him, she spurted out. My heart felt like it was going to stop. I told her this and she said it will not stop.

'It's broken then,' I said. She laughed.

'Do you know this because you're studying to be a doctor?' I spurted out.

'No,' was her answer.

'We had a good time that day. We both learnt a lot but now I have a boyfriend and he will be back soon, so I think we should say goodbye.'

'But I want to see you again,' I spurted out.

'Sorry,' she said.

'It would be best if you find another girl you like. It would be better if you go now before my boyfriend comes back.'

I was shattered and upset. Marilyn could see this and said goodbye and good luck. As I walked away with tears starting to fill my eyes I ran and jumped into the deep end of the pool to hit the bottom, wanting to stay there forever.

Chapter 10

Total Freedom – N.F.M., L.L., B.B., V.B., B.B.B.

Not long after getting over Marilyn, my next experience was obtaining my driver's licence. It was the most incredible freedom of my life. This freedom was immeasurable. I could come and go anytime, go anywhere, do anything, without relying on other people. All due to a little piece of paper, saying I can drive on a road in a car. For some time now, I had been putting money away, week to week, into my bank account.

Mum and Dad always said, 'Put a bit away from work for your car.' The time had arrived to buy my first car. Like all boys, I dreamed of a new car, maybe a V8 power machine, like Denis'. But it had to be a Holden for me. Dad always said that they are the best. I loved the early F5 and FB models best. Monaros were the top machines, but too dear for me.

At one of our happy hour times with all the family together for a change, Dad told us all the housing commission houses were being offered to the tenants to buy, with the current tenants first preference. Dad explained the housing commission plan. For tenants who wanted to buy the house they were in, they could put up a deposit, and also get credit towards buying the house based on the number of years they had been living in the house up until the time of sale.

This added up to a lot of money. Mum and Dad had no savings, six kids growing up, and Dad had three jobs. Mum was working part-time just to keep up with the living expenses.

After hearing Dad talk about the deposit money required, and how we might be able to save this amount in the future, it then occurred to me that I had enough money in my bank account to cover the deposit money required. Then with a little bit left over to buy an old car.

When I told Mum and Dad this, they did not believe me. I had to go and get my bank book to show them. Mum burst out crying, saying she could not take it. I knew she always wanted to buy a house, but said it's 'a dream only.'

I thought about how much they had done for us all, and told them that I was completely happy to give them the deposit money to buy an older car and slowly fix it up, giving me a hobby and something to do, tinkering with an old car and doing it up. I was looking forward to it.

Mum and Dad finally agreed. Mum seemed so much happier after this. She was about to give up her part-time job, and I started paying board for the bungalow.

I was now earning very good money from my apprenticeship. Dad's friend had an old FB Holden. Let's call it a rust bucket, but 'going cheap', it needed a lot of work. It suited me price-wise, so this was my first car. It got me around as I was slowly doing repairs to the body and motor, cleaned it up. New exhaust system of course, so as to have a good note from the old (138) motor.

This car got so much use, every day after work. Off to mate's places, going out all over the place. I loved driving, with the radio blaring out music, usually rock and roll, Elvis (I take after Mum).

I was going out every Friday night, picking up friends and dropping them back home – after touring beaches and the city – as I was the first in our group of friends with a licence.

In between my hobby of doing up my old grey FB Holden, work and friends, there were never ending hours in a day, or night, but eventually I finished my hobby. The old FB was now looking to me a 'work of art'. It was now painted a bright apple green colour, the latest colour out in the new

Holden range, with shiny mag wheels, change over red 18G motor upgrade with a new exhaust system, a beautiful sound system with a new radio and cassette, and big speakers all shaking the windows. Now I was happy with my old bomb.

With all this extra freedom, a couple of mates and I decided to go visit Denis and his family at Bonnie Doon.

His house was full of people. At the time, we were able to get a 'caravan on-site hire' opposite Denis' house. This worked out really well for about a week when we realised our financial situation was dwindling fast. So, as young men do, we stocked up on essentials: food, bacon, eggs, bread for toast, and slabs of beer. This should see us out.

Denis and his family would often call into the caravan park in his boat and take us out for water sports – skiing, body surfing. Barefoot skiing was Denis' favourite. 'Very hard to master.'

I tried but could not do it. Come the end of our stay, with little food left, we decided to go rabbiting, shooting them for food. Luckily, we got a couple to keep us going. Next day, my mate Bernie pipes up, as usual, 'What's up for breakfast?' he'd ask. I said, 'You have a choice – V.Bs or B.B.B. What's for lunch?'

Then he asked, 'V.Bs.' I spurted out. 'I'll start with B.B., followed by V.Bs. Then B.B.B. for tea,' was his order. We all agreed to the menu. It lasted us two days. Time to go home to proper food and lodgings.

Chapter 11

Virginia – N.F.M., L.L., C.E.3

With this new freedom that came with my driver's licence, I was meeting new friends. One of these new friends was telling me he how he went to a local church, which had a youth group starting up, and would I like to go along with him.

It brought back memories of the Salvos in the caravan. He told me the church was trying to encourage young people to join their church through music and dance. It sounded like a good idea. I liked music and dancing, especially rock and roll and 'Elvis Again'.

I met a new group of friends within this group, and enjoyed their company. There were so many different types of people: quiet types, loud types, and good-looking girls outnumbered boys. Great, I thought. We enjoyed every Friday night. Started with a prayer, and finished with a prayer with lots of good music and dancing in between.

I found myself drawn more and more to a girl named Virginia. She was a year older than me, and was what, again, I called drop-dead gorgeous. Her family were long-term members of the church. It was Virginia's vision to start the youth group, and she put pressure on the church parish to start the youth group. She was always involved in the church activities, and it had not been running for very long when I arrived on the scene.

I decided to tell Al about the church group of friends I had met. Al was very interested in joining, but I told him it was for older people than him. He understood this. Al and I would often talk about my experiences with this group in our happy hour within the bungalow. Al and I now rarely saw each other. I would always come home late. Al would be asleep, and we mainly caught up with one another occasionally on weekends.

As time passed, I admired Virginia for her devotion to the youth group and to helping others, organising events for the church and youth group. We only got to see one another once or twice a week, depending on whether I went to church on Sunday mornings or not.

I looked forward to Friday nights the most, mainly to see Virginia and to be close to her. I wanted to ask her to be my girlfriend, but she was always too busy fussing over everyone, thinking about her school and friends. It reminded me of Marilyn. Her friendship seemed to change when I offered to pick up her friends, then drop them off. It was a great time.

I thought we had known one another long enough to be able to go out together. So I asked her to the pictures together. Just us. Virginia said we could go to the pictures during the day on Saturday, but her dad would drop her off and pick her up. I thought that this was a start. After a couple of Saturdays, pictures only, her dad agreed. I could take her out for a drive during the day on Saturdays only.

This became my best day of the week. We went everywhere with friends. St Kilda beach, our favourite, to the snow lake mountain. It was great fun. We became very close. Her dad could see this and asked me to stay one Saturday when Virginia and her mum went shopping. To my surprise, he said to me his daughter had lots of friends, many male friends and I said, 'So do I.'

He smiled and said to take things slowly with Virginia. 'Do not get too attracted to her.'

I said, 'It is a bit too late, because I like her a lot.'

He said she had a bright future, and I should not get involved with just one person.

I said okay, not realising his point at this stage. We parted with him saying a prayer for all of us to have a better understanding of one another. It was not long after this talk with Virginia's dad that a new man arrived on the scene. He was a couple of years older than me and Virginia.

He had a beautiful new car compared to my old FB Holden. I felt things had changed between Virginia and me, and he was around more often within the youth group. I, not long after that, eventually got to take Virginia out on a Saturday night, but her dad said, 'No drive-in, go out for tea only and be home by 9:00 pm.'

After tea, we decided to go to a lookout over the beach. It was a cool night as we pulled up in a quiet carpark, looking towards the city lights over the beach area. It was very relaxing.

I felt the urge to kiss Virginia for the first time. She seemed willing and we were quickly kissing each other. As we kissed, her lips were so smooth and soft – sort of lubricated, I thought. Her lips had a taste to them – I could not work out what it was, but it tasted good. We then started touching each other all over. Me touching her breasts (woo) – she pulled back.

'We should not do this.'

'I know,' was my reply. 'But you look so beautiful.'

She then started to tell me that her mum and dad had always told her if this sort of thing should happen, she should always, always, 'Leave her clothes on, and pray for guidance.'

This thought quickly left my mind when, very slowly, she put her hand on my zipper and pulled it down and then popped the button above it. As she slid her hand inside my undies and clenched my penis, it was already growing so fast I could not stop it. Within seconds, it was protruding like the gear stick from the console of my car.

Virginia said I could touch her if I would like. She did not need to say it twice. Within a split second I put my hand up her dress and into her undies, fiddling around, trying to figure out what to do.

Virginia then put her other hand on top of my hand and slowly pushed my index finger into her vagina. It was an incredible feeling – it was so soft and smooth, with her pushing my hand up and down as if it were a puppet. Her body started to shake, as she rubbed me on the head of my penis with her thumb while clenching me even harder with her hand as her body shook even more. I could feel I was about to explode. Together we both seemed to explode. Virginia all of a sudden became wet all over my hand, and I could not control myself from exploding, as Virginia tried to stop me from making a mess by patting her hand over the top of my penis, but she yelled, 'It's going everywhere!'

Same here, I thought. *Has Virginia peed herself or what?* I thought.

Virginia said, 'It's called an orgasm,' as I grabbed my jumper which was next to us. What a mess. I could not stop myself; it seemed like forever, but it was only a short time.

Virginia was very apologetic, and so was I. After cleaning up a bit, she said she was very sorry, and I said the same. 'But you turn me on so much,' I spurted out, and she laughed.

What a start to a relationship, I thought. We kissed a bit more and I said to her I would like to touch her in the same way again, but she said, 'No. It's time we go home.'

It was quite a trip home. As soon as we pulled up at the front of her house, the front porch light went on, as if her mum and dad were waiting for us. Virginia said she was okay to go inside, and we best not tell anyone what had happened. As I watched her walk to the front door, her dad opened it and I waved to him, hoping he would not come out to the car. As Virginia went inside, her dad walked in also and closed the door. Thank god for that, I thought.

As I drove home I thought, what could I have done to avoid this mess? It should have been so good, my first time with what I thought was a real relationship. When I got home early for a change, Al was still awake, and I could not hold back telling him about my experience. He was lost for words when I told him what happened. He started laughing – he could see the funny side, which I did not see. The fact that a single touch could cause such a situation to occur. I told him how excited I got just kissing Virginia, that this had an effect on me I had not experienced before, and it was beyond my control.

It was not very long after this experience with Virginia, one Friday night, she asked me to take her home again. I was excited, until we arrived at her house, not far away. She told me she was now going to go out with the new boy (Sam it was). My heart felt broken again. I could not believe it. After her telling me this, I could no longer go to the church group meetings. Another low time of my life.

Chapter 12

Dr Wize's First Visit – N.F.M., L.L.

With all that was happening around me, I became aware of the possible consequences of my behaviour. I was aware of sexually transmitted diseases and possible pregnancy. I needed advice on the best way to deal with my relationships. All the talk amongst my mates about these subjects just made me more confused. I was trying to understand what could go wrong, being a sexually active young male and not very experienced. As Al and I had discussed getting advice from a doctor, not our local doctor, who knew everybody in our area, but a doctor miles away from us.

After going for a drive, I found a doctor's clinic about thirty minutes away from our house. This seemed to me to be far enough away from our area to explain my situation to him without him knowing any of my friends or family. I found it awkward to explain to him my feelings and concerns about sex. I soon realised I was so lucky again to have found this doctor by coincidence. The invaluable advice he gave to me on this day has guided me throughout my life. Basically, his advice was so simple, yet so complicated in application to life. He said to me, 'Son', and when an older person calls me 'son', I know I'm in for a lecture, but Dr Wize went on to say that his dad had explained like this to him, about life, this way.

Dr Wize said, 'When I was a young man, a long time ago…' He laughed, trying to lighten the subject. 'I was given the best advice a man could receive, and I am going to pass it on to you.'

My interest was now on high alert. He went on to say, 'If you live by this advice, you will be very happy throughout your life, as I have been. It's not as easy as it sounds, but it works very well when applied at the correct moment.'

As you know, the male body has a brain at the top of his head, let's call this H1. As a male matures, he discovers sexuality, the story of the birds and the bees, Adam and Eve, it seems pointless to explain these feelings. His body parts change dramatically when puberty occurs. It takes over, and you discover your penis does strange things at different times. Let's call your penis H2. This is where the important component of life comes into being. You must use H1 to control H2. Think with H1 before using H2. For any sexual encounter – sounds simple doesn't it? But chemicals in your body take over – testosterone, hormones and others.

As an example, you meet a very nice girl and you both have these feelings for each other, and want to have sex. Use H1 first. Do I use a condom to protect her from getting pregnant? Do I use a condom to stop me from getting an infection from her? You don't know her past history of sexual partners.

'Do you see my point?' he asked.

I told him this had not occurred to me before.

'This is why you must always use H.1 before H.2.'

I said, 'Does this mean I should always carry a condom around with me?'

He laughed and said, 'It would make good sense to have one close by. But it is not always the answer.'

This surprised me. He could see my surprise and then went on to give me another example.

You go out with your mates, and one says to you, knowing you always have a condom, I have this hot girl and she wants to have sex now in my car, can I have your condom? Do you give it to him or not? H1 needs to think very quickly, do I make a friend happy or not? Or do I tell him to go get himself one, even though I know all the shops are closed now. H1 decides that if you give it to him now, you will not have one for yourself, if the need arises.

I laugh and say I have a packet in my car.

'This is a good answer,' he said, 'but you left your car at your mate's house. If you did that, where do you stand?'

'I see your point.'

We both laughed. He then spoke about many occasions he experienced as a young man, who did not have the advantage of the condom as we do today. For him this made the H1 and H2 case even more important than today's situation.

We parted with him saying he wished he was my age now, and laughed about how good looking girls still turn him on, and wished me good luck with his advice. It was the best advice I could receive. After his advice, I felt confident enough to start using it. H1 and H2 would be tested many times over the years ahead.

My visit to Dr Wize shed a whole new light on my life. I often think back to my first sexual experience at the pool or with Virginia and how I would have handled it then knowing the H.1 and H.2 rule. It could have changed the rest of my life.

I decided to tell Al about Dr Wize's advice so he could learn from my experiences in such situations. Al could not quite understand the situation about being turned on by the simple touch of a female. I think he was too young to appreciate this experience. We spoke in depth about the H1 and H2 rule and how it will help him and me in the future. I must say here how wrong I was to assume Al's feelings (more on this later).

I asked Al again that this be our secret, between us only, and he agreed. It was not long after this discussion, a couple of weeks I think, on one of those rare occasions when we were all sitting at the tea table, all eight of us, having our family happy hour, when Al asked Dad about H.1 and H.2. I almost choked on my chop I was chowing into. I did not know what to say. Dad looked at me in a strange way. I thought, *quick, say something!*

'Al,' I said, giving him a whack on the back of his head.

'Ouch!' Al spurted out.

'Dad doesn't know my friends Harry 1 and Harry 2.'

'No need to hit Al,' Dad said.

Al realised his mistake and went along with my story, and Dad was asking all sort of questions about my friends as he did not know about them.

'Tell us about the two Harrys,' he said.

As all the sisters and Mum waited for my response, I started, 'Well, Harry No. 1 lives up the hill, we get on really well.'

Al started laughing, and I gave him a 'you're dead' look.

'He's got a good office job. Harry No. 2 lives down the bottom of the hill, don't see him very often.'

Al started laughing even louder and I started going red in the face, so I jumped up and said I had enough to eat, I've got to go and pick up H.1 – we're going to a mate's house. I thank Mum for a great tea, and say 'See ya later, sisters'. I am out of here, is all I could think of. The next day did I give it to Al, he said sorry, but I said he must be more careful of what he says in front of the rest of the family.

'Use H.1,' I said to him, and he laughed and laughed. I just love seeing the family laugh. Al's laugh is so addictive it makes me laugh. As Al and I talked further about H.1 and H.2 it occurred to us to have a code to better control our conversations around the family. We were lucky this time that H.1 and H.2 worked out okay. I told Al to be more careful about our bungalow talks and experiences when with family.

Chapter 13

My Shortest Job Ever – L.L.

Al and I spent many an afternoon at the ten pin bowling alley, opposite the mall, with not much else around at that time. This was a great way to meet up with friends and meet new people. It seemed like an entertainment place that, to me, would be there forever. But one day a sign went up, stating that the ten pin bowling was to close and a renovation to occur, opening up a new hotel for the area. This was about when I was eighteen years old. I thought, great for us locals – boy, was I wrong.

It was called the 'Colosseum' and it lived up to its name, very rough. I saw an ad for staff required to work there. I thought this would be okay for me to learn the inside workings of a hotel, but I was wrong again. I applied for a part-time job as a waiter with general job duties. Sometimes after work or on weekends, usually late in the day at short notice, when I was required. This seemed okay for a couple of weeks until one late afternoon, while doing my job, a group of young men (from my old McLeod Tech School days) were sitting around a table half drunk – one of whom I had had a run in with at McLeod Tech.

He, being a royal smart ass, said to me, 'Clean up this table, it's a mess.' And, as I started to clean up the table, putting rubbish into a bin, he said to me, 'And throw those old sandals in there too.'

I noticed he was bare foot and did not seem to want them anymore, so I put them into the bin, his mates all laughing now. I thought, am I being set up here? And sure enough, after about ten minutes, walking past the same table, the Smart Ass said to me, 'Where's my sandals?'

I said, 'You told me to bin them'.

'Bullshit,' he spurted, and started abusing me.

Lucky for me, the Colosseum had a bouncer, a big muscle-bound man, and he and I got on alright. He heard the commotion and came over asking what the problem was. I told him the story while the Smart Ass, carrying on about his sandals, says to the bouncer that I now owe him twenty dollars for these sandals, his mates all smirking, trying not to laugh. Bouncer Man says to leave it with him, and that he will fix this. We both go out back, I find the sandals – now in the big bin – and Bouncer Man takes them (very dirty and worn out) and attempts to wash and then dry them. We go back to Smart Ass, handing back the sandals, but he goes nuts, saying that he will not take them back now and still wants the twenty dollars.

Bouncer Man told them all in his very loud voice, 'ALL OUT NOW', flexing his muscles to show that he means business. I have seen him do this before and it does work.

As Smart Ass and his mates were escorted out of the hotel and into the carpark, drinking, I realised that they might be waiting for me to come out at the end of my shift. I went back inside to see Bouncer Man and tell him that they are in the carpark and that I think they are waiting for me. 'Let's see about this, come with me,' he said.

As we walked out the door together into the carpark, Smart Ass, leaning on the car, stands up straight away, as if to say 'I'm here, let's rumble'.

As Bouncer Man walked towards Smart Ass, he pulled out a note pad from his pocket – I thought he was going to pull out something else. He started writing down something and when he reached Smart Ass's car, he yelled to them, 'WHAT'S GOING ON HERE, MOVE ON NOW. GET IN YOUR CAR AND GO!'

Smart Ass argued that he was doing nothing wrong but Bouncer Man responded by saying 'Okay. I have your rego number,' showing Smart Ass his notebook, 'if anything happens to Arthur or his car, I will find you and you will be mincemeat. Now get going. Now!'

Smart Ass and his mates took the message, got into their cars and left. That night, I decided not to go back to this job, realising that it isn't worth the trouble that such a simple thing created.

The Colosseum did not last very long before being burnt down – I'm not saying Smart Ass did it, because there were lots of smart asses around at this time. I have never seen these men again.

Chapter 14

Lucky Phil, Lucky Me – N.F.M., L.L.

During the next couple of months, after Virginia's knock back, it was trade school week (one week block at a time). I happened to bump into Lucky Phil (his mother called him Lucky Phil – lucky with the ladies, I was told). He was a friend I met through another friend several months earlier at the trade school, Heidelberg Tech. He lived right next door to the school and I had seen him a couple of times at pubs and dances, always funny, always joking. He had an Irish accent and was always with beautiful girls each time I saw him.

He was easy to talk to, a good listener, and soon enough we started talking about girls. He said they are a complicated breed and I could not agree more, telling him about breaking up with Virginia. I was not going to talk about the break up, but he did not know her or any of her friends so I felt okay talking about it.

We sat and had lunch together that day and as we parted he said we should go out together on Saturday night. As I now had no plans I said how about next Saturday night and also planned where and what time.

Lucky Phil spurted out, 'Cramers, about 7.00.' – a hotel in Preston that was very popular.

'Sounds okay to me, see you there.'

He could tell I was a bit down about my experience with Virginia. As when he was walking away, he yelled out, assuringly, 'We'll have a good time, see ya Saturday.'

When I got home early, after bumping into Phil, I saw my neighbour Lionel (not always a happy camper), and started talking to him about trade school; he was at a university, doing a course in Business Management. I told him how much I enjoyed trade school, learning things, that I had a good teacher, made some good friends, and in talking about his friends and my friends, I mentioned Phil.

'Lucky Phil, you know him?' he asked me. Lionel said he went to tech school with him. 'We were in the same class.'

'What a coincidence,' I said.

'Watch out for him.'

'What do you mean?'

'He was always chasing trouble at school – cheeky to the teachers, chatting up girls.'

'What's wrong with that?' I asked.

'He was always the centre of attention and big-noting himself', Lionel said.

'This is not the Lucky Phil I know.'

'Wait and see.'

I did not tell him we were going out together on Saturday night; I decided to wait and see what happens.

I was now really looking forward to Saturday night, knowing a bit more about Phil, especially now that I have link with him and Lionel. I did not know yet if this was a good or bad thing.

On Saturday morning, I decided to go out and buy some new clothes to go out in. Got the lot, from shirt and pants to shoes and socks, and it felt great. As Al and I played my best rock and roll music in the bungalow and I told Al about the week's experiences, the time flew by and it was time to go out.

Chapter 15

Twin Lips – C.E. 4, Bingo, N.F.M., L.L.

Cramer's was a very busy dance pub; it had a live band playing the latest and loudest music, which was great to dance to, but it was very full of people, packed in like sardines, I thought. Luckily when I got there, I found a parking spot and eventually got inside after waiting in the queue for a long time. As I was walking around inside, looking for Lucky Phil, thinking he might be running late, I heard a familiar laugh: Lucky Phil. It was different to a normal laugh, it was a laugh you had to laugh at.

He was sitting at a big table with a couple of other mates I had seen at trade school and a couple of beautiful young women. Lucky Phil spotted me walking towards him, jumped up and yelled out 'Art! You made it. Sit down, meet my mates, Joe – oops sorry – ladies first.' He knew this would put a smile on their faces.

'This is Mandy,' who was sitting next to Lucky Phil and I thought she was gorgeous.

'Pleased to meet you,' I said.

'This is Teresa – not a teaser!' He spurted out, as everyone burst out laughing, including Teresa.

She was drop dead gorgeous, I thought to myself, and before I could say anything, she jumped up and said 'It's my pleasure to meet you'.

'Likewise,' I said. It was all I could think of.

'This is Joe and Tom, workmates.' Phil laughed as I sat down next to Teresa, being the only chair not occupied – how lucky was I? Lucky Phil poured me a beer from the jug on the table and emptied it into a glass waiting for me at my seat.

'Let me get another jug', I said, jumping up. 'Ladies, would you like another drink?' Thinking to beat Lucky Phil in asking them first, showing my friendly and easy-going nature. I got a yes from Mandy but an 'I'm okay' from Teresa. Lucky Phil jumped up also and said that he will help with the drinks.

As we waited at the bar to be served, Lucky Phil said, 'I think Teresa likes you'.

I asked him, 'How do you know this?'

Quick as a flash he said, 'When you walked in she said, "He is gorgeous".'

I thought, *was he pulling my leg, having me on, taking the mickey out of me?*

'You have something in common,' he said.

What could that be, I thought, then Lucky Phil spurted out 'motorbikes' with a big laugh. It was an addictive laugh and I could not hold back laughing.

'You're joking,' I said.

'No, it's true.'

As we returned to the table, the band fired up and the night got underway. In between jokes, laughter, drinks and dancing, Teresa and I got on like a house on fire. She talked about growing up on a farm with farm motorbikes and we talked about my bike at the time, which was similar to her farm bikes. She told me one of her brothers was looking after the farm with her mum and dad and that she wanted to work in the city, explaining that she worked in a shop not far away from where we were now. She was a bit older than me, very smart, knowledgeable and beautiful on top of all that.

Because we got on so well, I thought how lucky I was to meet her. As this great night was getting closer to closing time, I wondered if I could see her again. Not long after that thought, to my surprise, she asked me in front of everyone else, 'Can you take me home? I live not very far away.' I could not get my 'yes' out fast enough.

Lucky Phil jumped up to volunteer to take her home but Mandy grabbed Lucky Phil and pulled him back down into his seat, insisting that he was taking her.

Then Joe and Tom both spurted out about taking Teresa home. I felt like a loser, they were funny, a bit like Lucky Phil, both older and smarter than me.

Lucky Phil, then in his charming way, in a loud voice said, 'Why don't we let Teresa decide who will take her home.'

With this Teresa jumped up, my heart now racing, and spurted out, 'Let's go,' and grabbed my hand, pulling me up. 'See you all later,' she yelled out, my heart now racing 100 miles per hour.

As I drove the short distance to her flat, it was Teresa who asked if I would like to come in for a coffee, an offer I couldn't resist. Thinking with H.1, trying to control H.2, we parked outside her flat. It was very dark and late as we went inside and even after she turned on the light it wasn't much lighter. It turned out to be a very small two-roomed flat, like a motel unit with a bed, kitchenette and bathroom. Teresa instructed me to take a seat, saying that she will just be a minute, as she went to the bathroom and closed the door. She was right; within a minute, the door opened, except now she was in only a dressing gown. I was surprised. She then opened the front of the gown to reveal herself to me, with only undies on.

I could not believe what I was looking at, a beautiful body, her breasts with nipples as bright as red buttons. I started to shake, forcing my brain to think as my penis started growing as she came closer, then showing me something in her hand. This also surprised me, it was a condom. I thought, does she go to the same Doctor Wize as I did?

She sat on my lap and started to undo my pants. My penis popped out straight away, I was in a daze. Was this happening? How could I be so lucky as to be in this situation with a gorgeous girl?

As she slowly rolled the condom onto me, she said, 'Let's go to bed.' She then started undoing my shirt and as I stood up, my pants dropped to the floor, shoes off, my undies, shirt all off in a second, two steps to the bed and Teresa laid down, dressing gown still on, opened it up and slid her undies down over her knees with her hands, then her leg to push them the rest of the way down her leg and flick off. She did this while I was standing next to her at the side of the bed, thinking H.1, take all this in. I have never seen such a beautiful sight. Her body completely naked, not a hair on her body – nowhere – I thought this amazing body even more intriguing. I think she could see I was in a daze with my staring at her body. She reached over and grabbed my hand, as she said, 'Are you going to enjoy me?'

As I climbed onto her thinking H.1, this is your first real love experience, take it all in, I fumbled with H.2. I felt H.2 slide into Teresa, we were joined together, a feeling I will never forget. H.2 and H.1 could not have been any happier.

As soon as this feeling sank in, Teresa started moving what felt like her muscles within her vagina, clenching H.2. This made H.2 go crazy and I exploded into her. This seemed to go on for ages, but probably only minutes. As I seemed to collapse into her whole body, her breasts now squashed against my chest, she said, 'Stay inside me,' and we started kissing intensely.

She said she enjoyed kissing just as much as making love and asked me to use my tongue more, as she was using her tongue twisting and curling it in and out. It felt different and it got me excited again, as H.2. still felt her vagina muscles moving. She then said, 'I would like to be on top of you.' This was also very surprising to me.

As we separated, she slipped her arms out of the dressing gown. Sounded good to me, as we rolled over to swap positions, and I lay on the dressing gown, it was like silk, smooth and soft, like Teresa I thought. Teresa quickly positioned herself onto me, again this was an unbelievable experience. I could not resist holding her breasts, one in each hand, feeling her nipples for 'the first time'.

Experience for me, H.2. was so big and so deep inside her when she slowly tilted back, H.1. thought H.2. was going to break off. There was so much pressure, bending H.2. behind my body, I told Teresa it might break off, she laughed, and said it will never break off.

Teresa, with her hand on top of my hand, put it into H.2. and then pushed my index finger into her vagina, on top of H.2., this felt similar to the situation I had with Virginia – it was so soft, not enough room for H.2. and my finger I thought, but there was with her hand still on my hand and on top of H.2, slowly moving her finger up and down on what felt like the softest part of her vagina, she started to shake, similar to what Virginia did, I thought.

Then all of a sudden, Teresa yelled out a big sigh as a gush of fluid wash all over my hand. Again I was shocked and pulled away, Teresa said, 'What's wrong?'

I said, 'You've just wet yourself on me.'

She started laughing and said, 'You don't know what that was?'

As she started to explain I felt the fluid run down between our legs and onto the dressing gown. She then said to me, this is the best thing a man can do for a woman, as she straightened up still on top, we needed to talk about this she said.

'Is this the first time you have felt like this?' she asked.

'No!' I spurted out, 'I felt it before, but in a completely different situation.'

'Making love you mean?'

'Well sort of,' I said.

So, I told her about Virginia, and she laughed.

'Did you know what just happened?'

'Not really,' I said, 'did you wet yourself?'

She laughed out loud again.

'Is this the first time you have made love?' she asked.

'Well, not like this.' Teresa went very quiet for a couple of seconds, as she rolled over to the other side of me, I said, 'Did I do something wrong?'

'Not at all,' she said, 'that was fantastic for me.' She went on to say, 'You just gave me an orgasm, this is the best thing a man can do for a woman.'

'Can you explain to me an "orgasm"?' I asked.

She seemed surprised by my request, but went on to say, 'It's like when you get turned on and ejaculate, women do the same and it was called an orgasm.'

This blew H.1 away. 'No one has ever told me this before,' I said to her.

'You have a lot to learn,' she said.

'I love to learn.' We started laughing a lot. Touching one another all over was fun. She suggested we have a shower together. This sounded even better, if that was possible.

As we both squeezed into a small shower, Teresa said, 'Can you wash my breasts first?'

They were so firm and soft at the same time; her nipples stood out even more. As I was washing every bit of her with soap only, she insisted, when she placed my hand covered in soap on her vagina, I knew what to do with my fingers.

She started to shake all over again, H.2 got excited.

'Keep touching me,' she said pushing my hand way down her vagina until again she let out such a pleasurable sounding groan, I knew what had just happened. She was just smiling. As I tried to push H.2 into her 'not thinking with H.1', she grabbed H.2 very firmly, and said no let me wash you. She grabbed the bar of soap, with the other hand.

H.1 spurted out, 'What about a condom?'

'You won't need one this time.' She laughed, as she rubbed H.2 up and down with soap. Within seconds I exploded into her hand.

'It's okay,' she said, as she again laughed and laughed, now both of us laughing.

H.1 was out of control of H.2 again. *How could this happen?* I thought to myself.

I need another visit to Doctor Wize to sort things out. As we dried one another off, Teresa said she had to go out early in the morning to meet a girlfriend, so I should go home now.

I was so excited about what I had experienced tonight, she could do whatever she wanted. I asked her if I could see her tomorrow, and she said, 'Okay, say after lunch sometime.'

It was late when I got home, Al was fast asleep. I wanted to wake him and tell him what I had just experienced. I thought I just can't wait until the morning, but then thought, better go to bed. Sunday, I woke up early still excited from the night before. I woke Al up and started to tell him all about it. He was still half asleep as I started rushing, talking about Lucky Phil, boys and girls, but before I could get to the best part of the night, Al said he was going to go back to sleep. He rolled over and said, 'Goodnight'.

Not long after this, Mum yelled out lunch is ready, I wake Al and we go inside. With all of us at the table, I told the family about a nice girl Teresa I met last night, and that I was going to see her this afternoon. Then came too many questions with what I knew about her growing up on a farm, this made my mum and dad happy. After lunch I could not wait any longer – I jumped up and told Mum and Dad that I was off to see Teresa. I drove into her car park space, Teresa did not have a car, but her flat number was painted on the car park opposite. I notice Teresa and a man sitting out on the front porch area, next to Teresa's, with a small table and four chairs around it. They were having a beer and laughing, with music coming from Teresa's flat. They were winding down, after work I was told.

As I approached the man reached into an esky and pulled out a VB can and popped it open. He then stood up.

'Paulie, meet Arthur,' Teresa said, as he handed me the icy cold beer. As we shook hands, I noticed he was very strong, muscular, lots of tattoos, but spoke quietly, as if not matching his appearance.

Teresa explained they had been friends for a long time, and that he keeps an eye on her flat for her as he was looking for a job at the moment, and so was home during the day.

'Most days,' he also added.

Not knowing what else to say, I said to him, 'What's the motorbike over there in front of my car?'

'It is mine,' he said. 'A Harley. Best bike ever made.'

We discussed bikes: my little bike, his big bike, cars and music till it was dark.

Teresa said to Paulie, 'Time for us to go.'

'Let's have a coffee first,' she says to me, as Paulie goes into his flat.

We never got to have that coffee last time, I thought. When we went inside, Teresa turned on all the lights this time and I noticed a lot more about her flat than last time. Last night, the lights were turned down low, now I could see, and I was fascinated by her decorations on the wall opposite the bed.

Before I could talk about them, Teresa said 'give me a minute' and went into the bathroom, leaving me thinking, is this the same thing that happened last night?

Straight away all the previous night's thoughts came rushing back. H.1 was at overload. H.2 was starting to move. When the bathroom door opened, Teresa lowered the lights. First, dressed in her little white gown again, I knew what I was in for: another unbelievable experience.

I did not need any coaxing this time to remove my clothes, they were off within seconds. She again rolled on a condom, and as H.2 was as high as a kite, she could tell how excited I was, and said, 'Can we kiss a bit first?'

Me knowing what she was like while kissing, I obliged instantly. As soon as we again lay on the bed, my tongue and hers at war with one another, me holding her breasts, she grabbing H.2 tightly and started to rub me up and down as we kissed, it felt incredible and soon H.2 exploded. I could not control H.2. H.1 said, what, wait until I am inside her, but it was too late.

Teresa said, 'It's ok, let me show you some things I think you would enjoy.'

She slowly put her hands on my head and slowly pushed my head down over her breasts. I thought she wanted me to suck her breasts, but she pushed my head further down to her vagina.

'Kiss me there,' she said. 'The way you did just then, then kiss me using your tongue.'

I started to shake not knowing what was happening.

Teresa said again, 'It's ok' as she was moving my hands up and down on her breasts. I was using my tongue, kissing her vagina more and more, as she became more and more excited, I could feel H.2 getting excited and starting to throb again, then all of a sudden Teresa pulls my head up as she again lets out a grunting sound as her body trembled, H.2 exploded again.

Teresa let go of an amazing orgasm onto my chest it was like no other feeling I had ever experienced. She said thank you to me, and I said thank you to her.

As we kissed on her lips now, I asked if I could cum inside her. She immediately put her hand on H.2 and pushed inside her and she started to flex those muscles within her body, so much that within seconds H.2 again was throbbing, then exploding as we then lay side by side both very satisfied, I thought.

I said, when can I see you again?

Teresa said she was very busy the next couple of nights with her girlfriends. So, I suggested Wednesday.

She said, 'Okay, but make it early. Being a week night with work the next day, say make it about 6-7PM.'

I was looking forward to it, it was all I could think of. On Wednesday I rushed through everything at work so I did not have to work back. I got finished in plenty of time. Home by five, showered, dressed and arrived at Teresa's at exactly six o'clock. I was busting to see her again, H.1 thinking what new things will I learn tonight. As I knocked on the door, it opened straight away and I could smell her perfume through the wire security door as soon as she opened the solid timber door.

Teresa was looking fantastic, she even had bright pink lipstick on, looking like she had just finished putting on her makeup. I thought she did not need makeup, her natural beauty was enough to turn me on. I could not resist telling her how 'drop dead gorgeous' she looked, and she started laughing; another addictive laugh, like Lucky Phil's. She placed a kiss on my cheek, and then wiped the lipstick off my cheek gently with her finger, as if to say sorry I'll remove that. As it was still daylight, I noticed again all her decorations on the walls.

There was an unusual variety of things I had not seen before. Teresa could see my curiosity and said she collects things like that. Straight away, she asked, 'Would you like to go out or stay here?'

'Not a hard question for me to answer.' H.1 thinks she is all dressed up to go out by looks of things. So, I said to her, 'What would you like to do?'

To my surprise, she said let's put on some music and have a drink.

'Sounds great to me,' I spurted out.

For the first time, we sat on her small two-seater couch and talked for a while about our friends, bikes and cars. My joy at meeting her and her joy at teaching me about love, teaching, feeling and experiencing different things was exhilarating.

Out of the corner of my eye, I could not help but notice the items on her wall at the end of her bed. When I asked her about them, she said some of them are games. Toys I had never seen before, H.1 thought. Teresa started to kiss me on the couch; her lips tasted so good, it had like a flavour to it, I thought, I couldn't quite put a taste to it. This thought quickly disappeared when Teresa undid my zipper and said 'let's make love.'

H.2 was already starting to grow when we were kissing, H.1 trying to control H.2 – it was very difficult, but then Teresa said, 'let's jump into bed', and 'give me a minute' as she wanted to use the bathroom.

I quickly stripped off and got into bed – it was warm. Must have a heater, I thought. Teresa seemed to take a bit longer than before, so I called out 'are you ok?' just as the bathroom door opened.

She turned out the lights , but I could see she was naked in the moonlight from the bathroom window behind her – her silhouette was mind-blowing. H.1 and H.2, knew what was coming as she climbed on top of me. H.2 felt the condom roll on and H.1 had forgotten all about this, thankfully Teresa had not.

As I put my hands over her breasts, she positioned H.2 straight into her – this thrust of her body into mine was crushing me with warmth, softness and smoothness I had not felt before. For a split second H.1. thought something was different, but with each movement of her body H.2 was throbbing, then exploded.

Occasionally she bent over me, her breast touching my chest, to kiss me with that sweet tasting lipstick she was wearing, which made the kissing even better. Then she said 'roll over, your turn on top,' and as we did this in the pitch-black room, her perfume and makeup smell was irresistible.

We kissed a lot more, then she again put both her hands on my head, and I knew what this meant. Straight away I was kissing her vagina, this time it was different. H.1 thought the taste was similar to her lipstick in some way, because I was kissing her lips, I thought. H.1 was thinking her lips had had this effect on me.

As my tongue was now in overdrive, and H.2 was about to explode, again Teresa was trembling, I knew what was about to happen.

As Theresa grabbed H.2 and squeezed harder and harder, then she said keep going, until she exploded as she pulled my head up. Then in seconds H.2 exploded. I was gasping for air, when we both flung back, exhausted from our experience. How could this be even better than the last time, H.1 was thinking. As Teresa asked how that was, I said, I am speechless, words cannot explain how good that was, so I spurted out, 'It was even better than last time if that is possible.'

Teresa laughs and laughs.

'Last time was fantastic but this time, a bit different,' I said

'What do you mean?' she said.

'Well this time it came with tastes and flavours,' I spurted out.

Again, Teresa laughs and laughs. Teresa then said it's getting late, so we got dressed and Teresa said, 'You best go and wash up, you have lipstick on your face.'

I went into the bathroom and looked into the mirror and was surprised to see red and pink lipstick all over my face. H.1 thought Teresa was wearing pink lipstick, maybe I was wrong, or maybe it was multi-coloured or changed colours. Anyway, it washed off okay with soap and water.

When I came back out, Teresa blew me a kiss. I caught it and placed it on H.2 and she laughed. I asked her when I could see her again. She said she was busy until Saturday afternoon. This seemed so far away, but I said ok see you then. It was not as late as usual when I got home. Al was still awake. When I went into the bungalow, Al had the light on and was reading his magazines. Playboy, I think.

Thank God I did not have to do that anymore, I said to Al, as I was undressing and putting on pyjamas. As I pulled down my pants, my undies also fell down at the same time.

As Al and I were talking he glanced at my H.2.

'Bloody hell' yelled out. 'What is that?'

'What's what?' I said as I looked down at H.2. It was pink and bright red.

'Bloody hell,' I said.

'What is it?' he said.

I didn't know. It looked like some sort of a rash, Al said. Al jumped out of bed and said what have you been up to. H.2, still half aroused from the nights experience, H.1 started to go into overdrive.

I touched the red area with my fingers; it was soft and wiped off.

'What is it?' Al spurted out.

I put my fingers up to my nose. 'It smells like lipstick.'

'Lipstick?' Al yells out loudly.

'Shut up,' I shout. 'Keep it down. Mum might hear us.'

'How did that get there?' Al asked.

I did not have an answer straight away, H.1 was in damage control. Think, think, I started saying, then the penny dropped.

'I think I know what.' Al yelled out. 'Are you sick or something?'

'Something is more like it,' I said. It's complicated not knowing how to explain everything to Al, about how this may have happened. I think it might wash off, I'll go and have a shower.

'Mum's up,' Al yells out.

As I looked out the bungalow window, I saw the house lights were all out.

'Mum must be in bed by now,' I told Al. 'I'll give it a couple of minutes then go in shower.'

Al was very inquisitive. 'How does this happen to you?'

H.1 thinks hard about this question, and replied to Al, 'We played again tonight with Teresa and her friend. They had a tube of red lipstick on a roller type thing. I need to ask them tomorrow about this.'

Al looked at me strangely as if this did not answer the question.

I said, 'I'm going to have that shower now.'

As I started washing it off thinking back to Therese's flat, I am sure her lipstick was pink. The smell was sort of flowery, like rose petals – this was red and smelt like strawberry, it even tasted like strawberry. Then it dawned on me, this was the smell and taste I experienced, while kissing Teresa's vagina. How could this be? Surely Teresa would have told me about this. How did this and why did this happen to me? This must be why she took so long in the bathroom, I thought.

H.1 now thinking, did she put red lipstick on her vagina? I could not sleep, lying in bed trying to work it out. I eventually fell asleep, and when I woke up in the morning, Al was already awake, like he was waiting for me to wake up.

He was looking at me as my eyes opened up. 'Are you all right?' he asked, as a concerned brother would after seeing such a thing.

'It washed off, everything is fine,' I said, as I jumped out of bed quickly, got dressed and was off to work, before Al could ask too many questions. After work I went straight to Teresa's flat, still in my overalls, work clothes – not a good look. As I pulled into her car park, Teresa came over out of her flat with her girlfriend Mandy (Lucky Phil's girlfriend).

'What are you doing here?' Theresa yelled out, not her normal self.

I said, 'We need to talk.'

Mandy let out a laugh, similar to Lucky Phil's.

'Please Arthur,' Teresa said. 'We are running late. I will see you Saturday afternoon.'

'Ok. Can I give you a lift then?' was my response. Just then, a taxi pulled into the driveway.

'We are going out with friends and this is our taxi,' she said. 'See you Saturday.' She got into the taxi.

Come Saturday afternoon, I was nervous about asking Teresa about what had happened on Wednesday night. As I pulled into her car park, I again noticed Teresa and Paulie, sitting around the table, on the veranda. I could straight away see this could be awkward. As I opened my car door to get out, I noticed Teresa was going into her flat, and thought good timing. I did not want to talk to her in front of Paulie. To be polite I said G'day to Paulie, as I knocked on her door.

'She won't be long,' Paulie said. 'She's going to the loo, back soon,' he said. 'Sit down have a coldie.'

'Must be my shout,' I spurted out.

'Next time,' he spurted out.

It was a hot afternoon, and a coldie sounded good as he popped a VB in front of me.

'How's the job hunting going?' I said.

'Still looking,' he explained.

As we small talked about various things, eventually Teresa came back.

'Good to see you again,' she said. Followed by a big laugh from Paulie, which seemed strange to me, but straight away, Teresa said 'let's play some music,' as she grabbed my hand and lead me into her flat.

'See ya, Paulie,' she yelled out.

As she turned on the music – Elvis was her best – she said: 'Sit down. Want another coldie?'

'No thanks, I want to talk about Wednesday night. I thought you might let me tell you something.'

She started explaining our relationship. This surprised me as I thought this is what I wanted to say to her.

Teresa started with, 'I like you a lot. When we first met, I was very much attracted to you. I wanted to make love to you straight away.' This surprised me even more.

I thought about how lucky I was as she continued saying how much she enjoyed our relationship. She said she was still surprised that this was my first intercourse experience, and that this was not the same case for her. She could see the surprised look on my face and she stopped talking for a couple of seconds, trying to understand that this was complicated.

'I have had many experiences with many men,' she said.

I do not want to hear this. H.1 was now getting crazy again with all sorts of thoughts.

She then explained, 'I like to make love, and if I do it with someone like you, I enjoy it even more.'

Great, I thought.

But she went on to say, 'I enjoy teaching you different things, that included. What happened on Wednesday night? Did you enjoy it?'

'I sure did, it was amazing, but I don't understand how I got so much pink and red lipstick on me, especially the red lipstick,' I spurted out.

'Let me explain to you, this way: you know I liked to be kissed on my lips with your tongue.'

'So I enjoyed that too,' I spurted out.

'Well, I also enjoy being kissed on my lower lip the same way.'

'What do you mean "lower lip"?'

'My vagina,' she said. 'I put lipstick on my lower lips, as I prefer to call them. Red lipstick is my favourite. You did enjoy that, didn't you?'

'Oh, yes,' was all I could say as I could feel H.2 starting to grow. 'H.1 get control' I thought, as Teresa went on to explain our relationship. H.1 was going crazy, trying to take on all this information, and trying to control H.2 It was becoming more difficult. 'You turned me on so much – I can't control my feelings for you. I want to make love with you all the time,' was my response, not realising H.1 wasn't thinking straight, and maybe I should not have said this out loud to her.

'Look Arthur, it's like this: I do like you a lot, but I also like other men.' H .1 couldn't process thought.

As I was about to talk, she said, 'Stop, listen carefully to me. I enjoy your company, but I need my freedom also. I will not become your girlfriend as such, if this is what you are thinking.' (H.1 just killed H.2). Teresa could see the disappointment on my face. Then she said, 'Let me teach you one more thing.'

H.1 was going crazy again. What could she possibly teach me now after all the experiences we have had together? (H.2 started to fire up again).

'What do you mean?' was the only thing H.1 could come up with.

'Would you like to make love again?'

'Oh yes,' was the only thing I could say.

She started to undo my pants and shirt and said, 'Jump into bed. Just give me a couple of minutes.'

H.1 knew what was coming next as Teresa closed the bathroom door behind her. H.1 was going crazy thinking of what was going to happen now. H.2 was bigger than ever as the bathroom door opened. Teresa was in her gown, as beautiful as before. As she walked to the bed, it seemed a different sort of walk (I thought) for a split second. This was soon forgotten as Theresa sort of slid in bed next to me, then removed her gown and rolled on top of me, followed by rolling a condom over H.2. Starting to throb already.

She laid down on me and we started kissing, with her pink lipstick on her upper lips, and me not knowing what was on her lower lips. She slowly raised herself to a sit up position, her breast on my thigh muscles. H.2 was about to explode, when, to my absolute astonishment, one of her hands started to remove what seemed like a pearl necklace from within her lower lips. H.1 almost blew a fuse. What was happening here?

As she slowly removed this string of pearls, she placed them over and around H.2. With the other hand, she grabbed H.2 so hard H.1 thought H.2 was going to have those pearls embedded into it. The pearls reached the tip of H.2, then she laid them on my chest like a necklace. It seemed never ending. When the end finally approached, H.2 exploded. Teresa could see my shocked look and reassured me everything was OK.

'Now you can come again,' she said as she removed the pearl beads from H.2. All H.1 could do was nod a positive response. Teresa then inserted H.2 into her lower lips – H.1 could not get this idea out of my brain. It did not take very long before H.2 exploded.

H.1 was still in a daze as to what just happened. We both lay there, blinds on windows fully drawn to reveal daylight from bathroom windows shining onto the wall at the end of her bed, highlighting the various items hanging on the walls. H.1 could not resist asking what they were.

Teresa laughed out loud. 'They are my toys.'

'What do you do with them?' was all H.1 could think of asking.

'Well like those pearls next to you, I use them in a similar way.'

'No way,' I spurted out.

'Yes way,' was her response.

'I do not understand.'

She laughs again. 'This is why I like you so much.'

H.1 was in a daze again. H.2 was worn out.

'Look at it this way, Art. Part of what I am showing you now is me; I do tricks with my toys.'

H.1 starts to go crazy again. 'What do you mean?' I said.

'Well, see that board?'

'Dart board,' I said.

'Well, that's not a dartboard to me.'

'What do you mean?'

'See those ping pong balls on the tray under the board?'

'The balls with numbers on them?' I asked.

'Yes,' was her reply. 'Well, I use ping pong balls to try and hit the target board.'

Sounds like fun, H.1 thought.

'I'll show you.' As Teresa stood up, naked, and walked over to get four ping pong balls from the tray under the board, her body shone in the filtered daylight from the bathroom window. Her breasts stood out even more when she turned sideways to walk back to the end of the bed.

As she sat next to me at the end of the bed, she put a ping pong bowl into her mouth, and blew it towards the board. It hit the edge of the board.

'Good shot,' I said, and she laughed out loud.

'You have a go,' she said.

It seemed easy enough. As she put a ball in my mouth, she said, 'use your lips to force the ball out.'

Sounded easy, but I did not even hit the wall.

'It takes practice.' She laughed again. 'Let me show you another way.'

H.1 thought throwing it would be better. I could not believe my eyes when Teresa leaned back onto the bed and put a ping pong ball into her lower lips. H.1 went crazy again – what was happening?

As the ping pong ball flew across the bed and hit the board, my mouth dropped so much that she inserted another ping pong ball into it.

I spurted out straight away, 'What was that I just saw? It's impossible.'

'Not with practise,' was her answer.

'No way,' I said.

'Yes way,' she said.

We talked about this and other items on the wall. H.1 could not comprehend some of them. Teresa then said she had something else to tell me. H.1 was thinking there could not be anything else that could shock me as much as this has. Well, I was wrong again.

Teresa explained that she does these tricks for money. H.1 thinks, how does this work? Teresa could see the stupid, dumb look on my face.

'I have friends that pay me money to show them my tricks,' with a long pause, she said, 'you should also know I am paid to make love with them.'

H.1 felt like I was going to implode. This made my face go white (I am sure).

Teresa could see my reaction to this, and said, 'I know you might be shocked by this, but I must tell you now before it's too late.'

'Too late,' I yelled, 'it's miles too late. First, I love you.'

'You love what we have experienced together,' she said.

'Second, it is not the only reason to love someone. There is a lot more to true love than sex. Sure, it's a large part, but many other factors and feelings must be considered.'

'We have one or two things in common, when you are in true love, you probably need one or two hundred things in common. I will not have those factors in my life at this moment.'

H.1 was now so upset, H.2 dead. 'So, can we be friends?' I spurted out.

'I think it's best if we do not see each other again,' she said in a sad tone.

'That's impossible,' I said.

'No it's not. You are young, and you will meet someone else who you can teach whatever you want, to learn from our experiences,' she said as I got dressed, trying to hold back tears. (H.1 could not find words to explain my feelings.)

'Please can I see you again? I have money,' I spurted out. (I should not have said that.) Again, H.1 not working properly.

Teresa said, 'With me it's not about money, I really did enjoy your company.' After a couple of minutes of silence, she said, so softly, with a sad sort of a smile, 'I do not want your money. I am very busy all the time, maybe we might bump into one another in the future.'

'I hope so,' was all I could think of saying, as she slowly walked me to the door. She kissed me on the cheek and slowly wiped off the lipstick. Her eyes seemed to be glistening, or were they holding back tears, or was it my eyes, reflecting my holding back tears as we parted. I know it was both.

'Good luck,' she said as the door quickly closed.

Chapter 16

Bad Night – N.F.M., L.L.

As I returned to my car, H.1 was thinking how could a couple of weeks in a man's life change so much. Going from finding a girl of my dreams, experiencing everything a man could from a beautiful woman, to becoming absolutely devastated by the end of it. As I was driving home, H.1 was thinking, should I tell Al the truth about these couple of weeks. It was difficult, because I had just learned how dumb I was when it came to sexual experiences. I feel Al was far too young to understand this. (How wrong was I again to think this.)

Have I told Al too much already? H.1 started to think about his first sexual encounter with my mate's mum, then Marilyn the mermaid, then the third with Virginia. But, this fourth experience might've be too much for Al to understand. Though, it will stay with me forever.

When I arrived home early on a Saturday night for a change, just after family tea time, I went straight into the bungalow. Al was inside and could see straight away I was angry and upset.

'What's wrong, Art?' he said.

All H.1 could think of was, 'I just split up with Teresa.'

'The lipstick girl.' He laughed.

'Shut up,' I yelled. He could see I was very upset.

'What happened, Art?' he said in a calming way.

'It's complicated. I'll tell you one day,' I spurted out.

'Why not now?'

'I am tired. Go to sleep.'

'How's Big Red?' Al yelled out.

'Shut up,' I yelled again.

Al went very quiet and left the bungalow to go inside (I knew he would tell Mum and my sisters that Teresa and I were no longer together.) Just as well he did go inside, because I could not stop crying into my pillow at what just happened today. l fell asleep quickly I think because I started to dream about the week's events. It all seemed so real and I could remember tossing and turning, clearly seeing Teresa's body, feeling her all over my body, H.2 getting excited and exploding.

I woke up with a fright as I could feel H.2 throbbing and going crazy, growing, then all hell broke loose. I could not control H.2 – I was ejaculating into my PJs.

What a mess, H.1 thought. For a split second, back to the similarity with Virginia to what was happening now, except only me in bed. What did H.1 do to cause this, was I going crazy? I think I need another visit to Doctor Wize.

Due to me jumping up in my bed, Al woke up. 'What's wrong?' he said as I was trying to stop H.2 by holding it tight. This made it worse.

'I am going to the toilet,' I yelled out to Al as I rushed to the door holding H.2. Because it was dark, I opened the bungalow door and pulled down my PJs. It was too late, what a mess.

As I went back inside, Al said, 'Didn't you make it in time?'

What a good excuse, H.1 thought. 'No I didn't.'

'This happened to me too,' Al said with a laugh, meaning he needed a piss and did not make it outside in time.

As I changed my undies and PJs, Al said he was sad I split up with Teresa.

'Thank you, but it was the best for both of us,' I said, being half truthful. 'Go back to sleep, Al. I will go and wash these PJs, or Mum will be upset.'

'She wasn't with me,' Al said.

'Yeah, but I'm a bit older than you.'

Al laughed again loudly.

'Shush,' I said. 'You'll wake Mum up.' I headed out the door to the laundry.

Chapter 17

Betrayed – L.L., N.F.M., S.U.1

The next day – Sunday – lying in bed, thinking always about the weeks gone by, I thought of Lucky Phil and how I should go and see him, and thank him for introducing me to Teresa. I decided after lunch to go around to his house. I had not been there before, but Lionel told me roughly where he lived – not far away, and I knew his car.

It was easy to find, and when I stopped there seemed to be a party going on in the backyard with loud music. But I walked down his driveway, Joe, one of Lucky Phil's mates, came out of the side door and spotted me. 'Arty,' he yelled out. 'Come in.' He opened the gate in the driveway. 'Good to see ya mate, how you goin'?'

He was a real Aussie bloke, very friendly, like Lucky Phil.

'Not too bad,' I said.

'Come and see Phil and the boys out back.'

As we walked around the back of the house, Lucky Phil, Mandy, and about six mates of his were sitting around a big outdoor table, drinking VBs. A record player was blaring away.

Lucky Phil jumps up on seeing me. 'Arty! How's it hanging?' was his comment, and everybody burst out laughing.

I, thinking this was his way of joking, sat down.

Phil grabbed a cold VB from a big esky full of beer. Just what I needed, H.1 thought.

'How did you find me?' Lucky Phil asked.

'Lionel said you lived up this way, and I could probably find you by listening for loud music.'

Everybody laughed again. I was happy to break the ice, so to speak, by saying this. Good, H.1 thought. Mandy piped up and said, 'How did you and Teresa go the other night?'

Everybody started laughing again. H.1 was thinking where's the joke. Mandy caught me off guard. (H.1 – think what to say.) I spurted out, 'We got on really well.' Everybody laughed again.

'Got on top really well,' Lucky Phil yelled out. Everybody was now in hysterical laughter. Lucky Phil was bending over like he was in pain from laughing so much. This made me laugh – we were all laughing so much at one another – whether it was the beers, or each one's reaction to one another's laughter, I wasn't quite sure.

I started to get a funny feeling about Lucky Phil's comments. I asked Phil, 'What do you mean?' (H.1's usual reaction to a situation.)

He said, 'Mandy tells us you and Teresa "got on like a house on fire."' Everybody starts laughing louder than before. H.1 thought, now I cannot see the funny side of this. Lucky Phil could see I was not happy with this response.

'Mate, mate,' he spurted out. 'Girls talk about everything.' He turned to Mandy and winked to her. H.1 was now getting a really bad feeling.

'What do you mean?' I spurted out again.

'Mate, mate, we are all mates here. We all get on really, really well,' said Lucky Phil. H.1 thought, I can see that. He went on to say, 'Even the girls are mates, if you know what I mean.'

'Not really,' I spurted out.

'Let me put it to you this way.' (Nobody was making a sound. They were all just looking at me as if I was an alien from another planet, H.1 thought).

Phil said, 'I like you, mate. Joe, Bob, Mandy, the rest of us – we all like you, and thought you needed to meet a "nice" girl like Teresa.'

H.1 started to go crazy – I jumped up so fast everyone seemed to fly back into their chairs and I grabbed Phil by the neck with both hands. 'You mongrel,' is all H.1 could think of. Within a split second all his mates were pulling me off him. H.1 was so angry. Anger I had never experienced before.

As they grappled me to the ground – Joe, the biggest, sitting on my legs – they all started laughing again. Phil had a serious look on his face, holding his neck, as if his head was going to fall off.

'You bastard,' I yelled out.

'Calm down,' was his reply.

'You set me up,' I screamed, and the laughter got louder. 'How could you do this to me?'

'Mate—'

'Don't call me mate, you bastard.'

Upon hearing and seeing all the commotion, Phil's dad came running over to us. 'What the hell is going on here?' he yelled.

'All under control, Dad. Go back inside,' Phil said.

'Are you alright?' Phil's dad asked.

'No I'm not,' I yelled back.

'He'll be OK in a couple of minutes,' Phil tells his dad. 'Dad, Mum's calling you. Go back inside.'

As his mates lifted me up, I again lunged at Phil. He grabbed me by the neck as his mates held my arms. 'Sit down, loosen up,' said Phil.

'I don't have much of a choice, do I?' I spurted out as his mate set me at the opposite end of the table.

Mandy looked at me with a smile, as if to say, I like you (H.1 thinks, am I dreaming?). Phil started to explain things. 'We are all mates, and we all love Teresa,' and then quickly follows with 'also Mandy.' Mandy gave Phil a dirty look. (H.1 was thinking does Mandy do the same thing as Teresa?)

Phil could see my looks to Mandy and quickly said, 'Do you have something to say, Mandy?'

H.1 was thinking, what could Mandy say to help me understand her betrayal to me by telling Phil everything about Teresa and me.

Mandy started by saying, 'I like you.'

Phil did not seem to react to this, which surprised me. H.1 thought, what the hell is going on here. Then Mandy said another thing I will never forget. 'I taught Teresa everything she knows.'

H.1 went crazy again. Everybody started laughing, at the look on my face, I guess. Even Phil smiled. At first, I wait for my reaction to what Mandy said to sink into my head, and my response to her surprising statement. H.1 automatically put a smile onto my face.

Lucky Phil jumped up. I thought he was going to strangle me again. Instead, he hugged me. I had never been hugged by a man before, except dad. H.1 sighed with relief at his response.

'Let's go for a walk,' he spurted out.

As we walked around the block, he told me, 'Teresa is a very special woman and she does like you a lot. She was surprised you were a virgin.'

I froze. Phil could see the look on my face. 'Don't worry,' he said. 'Teresa and Mandy talk about everything to me, just so you know this. We didn't tell the boys that this was your first time with sex.'

H.1 straight away spurted out, 'Not my first time with sex. I mean, I have touched a woman before.'

'Right,' said Phil, 'but not like Teresa, right?'

That's for sure was all H.1 could think of.

'Listen, Art. Teresa really, really enjoys herself. She is very smart, has big plans for her life. At this stage, you should back off, let her go.' (H.1 was taking all this in – I did not want to hear this.)

Phil explained that Teresa was a 'nymphomaniac'.

'I have never heard this word before,' I said.

'Let me explain it to you: Teresa loves making love. Enjoys it more than many women do. This is what makes her so special – her and Mandy are the same. Lucky me,' he spurts out. 'And we only enjoy one another's company – relationships. Do you understand?'

All H.1 could do was nod, as I tried to understand all I had just been told. As we walked back to Phil's backyard, the boys were laughing, not at me now but at Mandy's dancing on the tabletop. She quickly jumped down when she saw us coming in.

'Just dancing,' she spat out. Phil laughed out loud.

'Looks like you need another coldie mate,' Joe yelled out.

'Make it two,' I said. The first one barely touched the sides. As I sculled it down within seconds, all the boys cheered. The next one went down a bit slower, and, by the end of the day, I was what you call 'rat shit'. Phil and Joe could see I was very drunk.

'I'll take you home,' piped up Phil. 'You live next to Lionel, don't you?'

'Yeah' is about all H.1 could say. All the boys were laughing. I could not see the funny side of this.

Lucky Phil took me home, and Joe took my car home (dropped it off thank God).

Phil told Mum I was not feeling very well. She could see that, I'm sure. Mum told Phil to put me in bungalow out back. The last thing I remember this day was Mum telling me off. 'Very angry,' I thought.

Chapter 18

Dr Wize: Second Visit – L.L

The next day (Monday), when my alarm went off to get up, I could hardly move. I felt so sick. I told Al to tell Mum to ring my boss, Denis, and tell him I was sick. 'Never before done this before now'.

My mum came out and took a look at me. She knew exactly why I was sick – she said she could smell me from the door of the bungalow.

'You deserve this,' she yelled out, and 'I hope you learn from this.'

'Yes, Mum,' was all I could get out of my mouth, with my tongue feeling like a large foam sponge, unable to move. Mum told Al to go and get me a bucket from the shed.

'Why?' he yelled out.

'You'll see,' she said as she stormed out. That bucket it sure did come in handy. Al, being on school holidays and at home, could not believe how sick I was and suggested I go see a doctor. 'Doctor Wize,' he laughed.

As the day went on, after a couple of vomits later I started to get a little bit better. Al and Mum kept checking on me, asking if I wanted food or drink. This did not help, as I lay in such a dizzy, very sad and sorry, half-conscious state. Al was in an out, asking lots of questions. I could not even think properly with H.1 hurting so much.

Eventually night arrived, which helped a bit because it was quiet and dark. In the morning Mum woke me up. 'You're going to work today,' she spurted out.

'I still feel very sick,' I replied.

'Denis is going to be very upset with you.'

'Tell him I am sorry.' As I lay in bed, I felt H.2 was not quite right – sore and stinging a bit, I thought. Nearer to lunch time, no food or drink yet, I got up and told Mum I was going to the doctors.

'A doctor won't help,' she spurted out, but, not long after this, I felt I had to go see Doctor Wize. Doctor Wize was happy to see me and asked how his advice was working out.

'Like you told me, it is not as easy as it sounds.'

He laughed and then asked, 'What can I do for you today, Art?'

I explained how sick I was after drinking so much beer, and he explained the consequences of too much alcohol in the body. The results of this surprised me. 'Never again,' I told him. I then told him H.2 was not feeling normal – it stung a bit when I urinated, and was sore sometimes.

'This does not sound too good,' he said. 'Give me a look at H.2.' He laughed.

I was embarrassed but I had to show him.

'It's not an STD,' he said straight away.

'Thank God,' I said.

'Maybe too much alcohol in your system, or too much use by H.1 again,' he said, laughing. 'STDs can happen to anybody who is sexually active.' He explained that condoms can help stop this from occurring.

I told him that sometimes I use condoms.

He said, 'Even when using condoms, a disease can still transfer some person to person via bodily fluids, or by touching various areas of the body with hands and transferring organisms or disease by hand.' This surprised me. 'You need to be very careful,' he said, and explained in detail the problems.

H.1 was now thinking about 'twin lips', but I dare not mention this to Doctor Wize. (He would probably be shocked, I thought.) On my way home, I was thinking of Virginia. I heard on the grapevine that she had become sick. An STD, I was told.

She was now regularly going out with Sam, the new man in her life after me, at the youth group. I decided to give her a phone call. Her dad answered the phone, he was not very happy and told me to 'Never to ring here again'.

I said, 'Why?'

'You got Virginia very sick,' he said.

'No way,' I said. He did not want to know anything about this. 'Let me explain,' I said.

He said, 'This is impossible, goodbye,' and hung up. This made me angry, and I went to see one of my old friends from the youth group, another 'Phillip'. He told me how things changed a lot when Sam arrived on the scene. He started to control everything, including Virginia, and the youth group fell apart and ended. 'I heard that Virginia is now having a baby.'

'No way,' I said.

'No one has seen her for ages.'

At the end of this week, on my way home from work, I decided to call in to Lucky Phil's house and tell him about my visit to Doctor Wize. He was out the back having a beer by himself, music down low. I knocked on the side gate and yelled out 'Lucky Phil, is that you out there?'

As he opened the gate, he said he was glad to see me, and come and sit down, grab a coldie. He said he wanted to apologise for our last get together on Sunday, and how it got out of control.

'It's OK,' I said. 'I've learned a lot.' Lucky Phil laughed out loud. I missed his laughter. I asked, 'How are Mandy and Teresa going?'

He seemed a bit down. He told me, 'They have moved on.'

'What do you mean?' I spurted out.

'Gone North,' he said. 'They left yesterday, gone to the Gold Coast. I'll miss them,' he said in a sad way.

'Are they coming back?' I asked.

'They don't know. It all depends on them finding a place up there,' he spurted out.

I told Phil about Doctor Wize's comments, and he said Mandy and Teresa were very careful about things like that, and they had never been 'sick' in that way. 'Thank God,' I spurted out.

Phil just shook his head; I could see he was really down. I suggested we could go up there to see them come Christmas holidays. He then became more interested in our conversation. 'I've always wanted to go up there,' I spurted out. 'Let's work on it. Time for me to go home for tea. Sorry to hear about Mandy and Teresa. Be in touch soon to plan our holiday,' were my parting words.

Chapter 19

Words – L.L., N.F.M.

After talking with Lucky Phil, with the ladies gone North, I decided to spend more time with family, Al, my sisters and friends.

Al and I were now be spending more time together in the bungalow. I started telling Al about my experiences – he was amazed at them. Him asking questions, me trying my best to answer them. Then, one Sunday at family happy hour tea, Dad asked Al, what Art has been teaching him in the bungalow (Dad has noticed us spending more time together).

Al spurted out, 'tell Dad about your orgasm.' (Trying to show he was learning something new.) I whacked him on the back of the head (like I've done before) as Mum and Dad nearly choke on their food.

'Al,' I shouted out. 'It's called "organisms" – "germs", you idiot.'

'I'm not an idiot,' Al yells out.

'Well get it right,' I said as Al realises he has said the wrong thing.

Dad says out loud, 'That's enough, you boys.'

Mum and my sisters now stopped eating, looking at us boys arguing.

'What's going on, Arthur?' Dad said, in a stern voice.

'I tried to explain to Al about organisms, germs, diseases, things like that.'

Dad smiled, and gave me a funny look. My sisters pipe up, 'What about them?'

'They ask, you tell them, Al,' I said. 'Explain about germs and diseases.'

'Always wash your hands,' he spurts out, and Dad and I crack up laughing.

'What else does Art teach you?' Dad asks Al.

'What was that word last week, Art?'

H.1 thought, oh no, what's he going to say now.

'Contraception,' Al spat out, with a whack behind the head again by me. 'Ouch!' yelled Al.

'Al, the word was 'contraption'. Machine digger, you know' – was all I could think off straight away – 'that contraption I use at work with Denis. The drainage machine.'

Dad looks at me strangely again. 'What else did Art teach you about, Al?'

'Um, masturbation,' Al said as he ducked his head and laughed, expecting a whack again. I got the feeling dad could see a common element to these words.

'Explain that one, Art,' said Dad. My sisters were all ears.

'Al, it's 'master the motion' – dancing to a beat, like the big red dance I taught you. Remember?'

Dad smiled, I now thought he was onto our words. I gave Al another whack behind the head now as he was laughing at my answer. (Not expecting that, were you, I said.)

'Al,' I shouted out. 'Get it right, words are very important. If you get them wrong or mixed up, it can do a lot of damage to people.'

Dad started laughing. Mum smiled, and my sisters were now laughing. We were all laughing at one another (great feeling at last). Dad went on to say to my sisters, 'Learn all you can at school. Words are so important to learn about life and experiences. Even I am still learning words,' and laughed.

Not long after this Al said he had something to tell me. As we sat in the bungalow, he did not want me to be shocked or upset. (He did not know what this could do to me.)

Then he spurted out, 'I'm going to be a father.'

'Bullshit,' I spurted out.

'It's true. Kay and I love each other very much, and we have decided to get married.'

'You're joking,' was all I could think of to say. 'You're only seventeen. How could this happen? Did you not listen to my H.1 and H.2 advice?'

'It worked sometimes,' Al spurted out. 'But not all the time,' was his response.

'Have you told Mum and Dad yet?'

'No,' Al said, 'I wanted to talk to you first.'

'This will affect the rest of your life, Al.'

'Yes, I know it will. Kay and I have thought a lot about this, and she would like to have a baby.'

Kay being one year older than Al, eighteen, it was OK for her to get married. But Al went on to say 'We need to go to a court.'

'A court,' I spurted out.

'Yes. A judge will need to hear our case and decide yes or no to our marriage.'

I could not believe what I was hearing. 'This is all too much for me to take in, Al,' I spit it out. 'What will Mum and Dad say? What about Kay's mum and dad? Are you one hundred per cent sure Kay is pregnant?

'Yes, she had a test last week at the doctors.'

At this stage, Al had left school at sixteen, got a job in a factory, and was saving money, as I did. Kay was also working in an office.

Al said, 'We have some money saved, and this will help us survive.'

At this stage, I must say, I had met Kay on several occasions – usually at a party with Al, or at home with our family. Looking back at this, I should have realised her love and devotion to Al was strong. She was always holding onto his arm (something I had not experienced), always polite, very caring about our sisters – I never heard her swear or raise her voice in anger. Kay got on really well with my two youngest sisters, now twelve and nine (both soon to be aunties and me, an uncle – and four other sisters also aunties).

Al said 'We are going to tell Mum and Dad, and Kay's mum and dad this coming weekend. We'll get together for tea on Saturday night.'

I was so overwhelmed with all this. 'How could this all work out?' I said to Al.

'We will work it out on Saturday as a family,' he said as I sat on my bed, opposite Al's bed, in total shock. Al could see my face change colour and said, 'Are you OK?'

I could not talk (thinking, how this is going to work out?).

I said to Al, 'There are alternatives when a lady is pregnant.'

'Don't even think about that,' Al spurted out. 'We have made our decision to get married. One hundred percent.' (Never in my wildest dreams could I have heard this from my brother.)

I was not at home for tea on Saturday night – I had to get out, not be there. It would be complicated enough without me there. When I did get home, about midnight, the light was still on in house. Kay's mum and dad's car was still out front. I thought I'd better go in. Everybody was sitting around the table. Al stood up straight away and said to me, 'Kay and I are getting married.'

I felt my jaw drop to the floor. Mum and Dad and Kay's mum and dad were smiling; I knew everything was now OK.

Mum and Dad loved children, and so did Kay's mum and dad.

'Now we're all about to become grandparents,' Dad spurted out. Dad explained to me, as best as he could, about how 'not happy' he was about the circumstances, but 'very happy' for the marriage. Not long after this, a court visit was organised, because Al was under eighteen. A judge heard how much they loved one another from both mums and dads. The judge made a great decision to give permission for Al to marry Kay. Next thing, they were married in a church, me as the best man – what a day that was.

Chapter 20

Holiday??? N.F.M., L.L., S.U.2 (Bigtime)

As the time got closer to Christmas holidays, I again suggested to Lucky Phil (now over Mandy and Teresa) that we go to the Gold Coast for holidays. At first he was not so keen, but after talking to Joe, Tom and Lionel, convincing them to go with us to share costs, he decided to go. (Five of us in the old 'FB' Holden – how would we go, I thought.)

As we got to within one week of going, (after Christmas with the family) Tom pulled out, saying he had other plans. So, now down to four of us. At least not so crowded now, I thought. Lucky Phil, Lionel, Joe and me, four-way sharing costs for fuel and accommodation.

I said to Lucky Phil, as a joke, 'With my car bright green, Mandy and Teresa might find us.'

He laughed, his usual addictive way. 'I hope so,' he said. Not much thought went into planning this trip. We all just threw a couple of things into the boot: esky of course, bathers, some clothes and maps to Queensland, and off we go. Well, we determined to get there ASAP – which meant no stop over. Straight driving, I think it took about twenty-two hours to get there.

On the way, (about mid-NSW) as it was nearing dark, we saw a hitchhiker. Lucky Phil yelled out 'Stop, let's give him a lift.'

'Not much room in the back,' I said, with Lionel next to me, Tom and Lucky Phil in back seat.

'Nah, we'll be alright,' yelled out Lucky Phil. We turned around and went back to the hitchhiker. When we pulled up, Lucky Phil jumped out. 'What's your name?' he spat out.

The hitchhiker said, 'Bob'.

With the windows down, I asked 'Where you are going?'

'Heading to Gold Coast,' was his answer.

'Bullshit,' piped up Lucky Phil. 'So are we. You're so lucky – jump in,' Phil said.

Bob noticed the back seat. 'Not much room,' he said.

'If you nurse your backpack, we'll be OK,' Phil spurted out. Not long after picking Bob up, lots of chatter filled the back seat. With the music now turned down low, Bob asked if could he light up a cigarette.

'Of course,' spurted out Lucky Phil.

'Would you like one?' he asked Lucky Phil. 'Does anyone else want one?' he asked.

Lucky Phil and Joe said 'yes' straight up. 'Not me,' I said, 'I tried … once, but never liked it.'

'No thanks,' said Lionel, next to me, now nearly going to sleep as late-night approaches.

Bob lit up a cigarette – not a normal one. His ones were the roll-your-own type. Lucky Phil asked, 'Are they cheaper?'

'A lot,' said Bob. Lucky Phil and Joe jump at the opportunity to try a roll-your-own cigarette. Well, with three smokers in the backseat, music now blaring, Lionel now snoring next to me, and a car full of smoke, I wound down my window to get some fresh air, even though now I was a bit cold. I had never smelt this type of smoke before. All the laughter from the backseat overpowered the music. It was time to stop and fuel up, have a break. As I pulled into the garage to fuel up, I was feeling pretty happy and laughing with the boys – I could not stop laughing at them laughing, I did not know why.

We eventually took off again, and things quieted down a bit. Lucky Phil and Joe were asleep, Lionel was still snoring next to me, and hitchhiker Bob started talking to me, with the music now off.

Bob told me how each year he goes up to the Gold Coast and has a great time – partying is easy, everybody wants to party on the beach, especially at night, even in hotel rooms, everywhere. It sounded great. I could not wait to experience it. He seemed a bit older than us.

He then asked me if I wanted a smoke and I said I don't smoke. He said his smokes are 'special'. I did not understand this and said 'what do you mean?'

'These smokes make me happy,' he said.

'I am happy already,' I said.

'That's because you had some of our last smoke,' he said.

'No, I did not,' I spurted out.

'You were very happy about an hour or so ago, weren't you?' he said.

'Yes, I was laughing with you all.'

'No, you were laughing because of the smoke,' he said.

'No way,' I said.

'Yes way,' he said.

'What does this?' I asked.

'It's called marijuana, a special type of "tobacco",' he said. I have heard of this but know nothing about it. 'Let me explain,' he spurted out. He said he makes his own cigarettes and sells them on the gold coast. 'My backpack is full,' he spurted out.

'No clothes,' I said.

He laughed. 'I usually come home with clothes and lots of money.' He laughed out again.

We talked about his experiences for hours as we drove closer to the Gold Coast – it helped me to stay awake, as I was starting to get very tired. With a couple hours to go, I stopped and woke up Lionel, knowing he has had the most sleep. 'You drive, I'm buggered.'

Lionel was rapt to drive my car, he always wanted to drive my car. He had a licence but no car. Many times he asked, but I said no. So today I made his day.

As Bob and I now went to sleep, I hoped Lionel would get us there in one piece. After what seemed like two minutes of sleep, but was actually two hours, Lionel yelled out, 'we're here.'

Coolangatta, Queensland. Everyone woke up.

'Best place,' Lucky Phil spurted out as we watch the rolling ocean crashing into the white sand. It was such a beautiful picture to see, I thought. We made it.

It was early morning, not much happening. A couple of people were walking along the beach, the odd runner on the edge of the water line. We all piled out of the car, looking for somewhere to eat. Everything was closed. Not very welcoming at all, I thought. We thought the place would be buzzing. Bob spurted out 'things will liven up soon,' and offered up smokes. 'Anyone?'

Joe and Lucky Phil were straight into this offer. Lionel looked at me, and I shook my head. 'No thanks.'

Lionel said, 'No thanks.' Then Bob opened up his backpack – a big one – full of cigarettes only (I thought he was kidding me earlier when he told me this.)

'I need food first, or at least a coffee. A strong one,' I spurted out.

We sat on the foreshore, Bob thinking about party places, pointing at the best spots. As the laughter got louder and louder, Lucky Phil 'stands out', I thought. Lionel spotted some movement at one of the coffee shops in Main Street. 'Coffee anyone?' he yelled out.

'Boy, do I need a coffee,' I said. We all headed off to check it out. As we got closer, the smell of coffee got me fired up. It wafted around the shop. I yelled out to the guy setting up the chairs outside, 'Open now?'

'Won't be long,' was his response, as he set up a table for us on the footpath outside the shop. 'Sit down here, won't be long.'

Soon after, a beautiful young waitress appeared. 'Can I get you guys anything?'

Straight away Lucky Phil spurted out, 'You can give us something,' and burst out laughing, along with Joe, Bob and Lionel. I could see she was embarrassed as she turned and walked away. I thought, we are not going to be served here.

Just then another setting-up guy came to us – a very well-built muscular guy, and said, 'Can I give you guys something?' in a very serious, strong tone of voice.

I looked at Lucky Phil, and in typical Lucky Phil style, he piped out, 'Mate, we were only mucking around. Joking, take it easy, fellows.'

The polite man spurted out, 'Settle down a bit.' I gestured to the polite man with two fingers, pretending to draw a drag, as they call it, on a cigarette, and pointing to my mate, still laughing, he got the picture and walked away. About ten minutes later another lady waitress, a lot older, asked 'Would you boys like to order now?'

I was thinking of food, but now I was thinking just about getting a coffee; I had heard about what could happen with food when you upset the staff. 'Make it five coffees for starters,' I said politely.

'Good choice,' the lady replied, as if to know what I was thinking.

'I want food,' Lionel yelled out.

'Yeah.'

'We will work on that,' I said as the waitress walked away after handing us the menu. I explained to Lionel my thoughts, and he could see my point. The three boys were now laughing and joking about what could be put in food. No food here for us, that was for sure.

After our coffees Bob said, 'The pool hall up the road should be opened soon. I know the owner, he will look after us.' Off we go.

'I'll feel better if we have breakfast somewhere else,' I said. The pool hall was big; lots of tables – a bit smelly for me, but Bob knew the boss, and said g'day to him. As they chatted, we sat down.

'Is the kitchen set up?' Bob spurted out.

'Give us half an hour. Have a game on us,' he said. The boss said we were the only ones in the place, and that bloke 'Bob' was a good friend of his. Within half an hour or so, the place started to fill up with other young manly men, and the odd girl or two; the place started to feel more welcoming. Having other people around laughing, hearing the music playing, I got the feeling the place was coming to life. After a couple of games of pool it was time to eat. I was so hungry, we all ordered up a Big Breakfast, and it all disappeared pretty quickly. Luckily, before we were ready to leave, Lionel asked the boss man where a good place to stay was. He said most of the cheaper places were booked out. He told us to try the upmarket high-rise places.

After many phone calls, we got three nights at a good high-rise building overlooking the beach. A bit more expensive than we were planning, but there was no other choice.

Bob piped up. 'Did you get a place to stay?'

Lucky Phil spurted out, 'Yep, up there on the beach hill, high rise. Lionel's got the details.'

Bob pointed out to Lionel the way to find our apartment. Bob then said he was off to catch up with some of his mates, and we might see him tonight at the pool hall. That was the last we saw of him.

We eventually found our apartment – it was perfect. Cost us a packet, but worth it. The view along the beach was breathtaking. We all crashed and had a good sleep. By very late afternoon, Lucky Phil woke us all up. 'Let's party,' he spurted out. Lucky Phil wanted to go to the pool house to see Bob – he liked his smokes and wanted to buy some. With us playing lots of pool, drinking lots of grog, talking to the locals, Lucky Phil spotted the boss and asked him if Bob had been in. The boss told him, 'Bob starts here and then goes up North. We may not see him again.'

We stayed only a short time after this news. Luckily, because we were all a bit pissed by now. Lucky Phil spat out he saw a sign in the apartment block advertising a karaoke night at a pub. 'Let's go there,' he spurted out.

After asking around the pool hall locals about the karaoke place, we finally got on the right track. 'It's about five blocks away from here,' a guy told us. Off we went, as we walked to this pub, we could not help but notice the streets were now full of young people everywhere, and loud music coming from the beach. The place was old lit up like a circus, I thought. It felt really alive, buzzing. We eventually found the pub – a big place, very busy, with people everywhere.

'Maybe it's full,' I spurted out.

'There's a queue to get in.'

'Great,' Lucky Phil yells out.

'Look at all the chicks,' Joe yelled out. We queued up straight away, Lucky Phil on to a group of girls in line. The four of them together started laughing straight away.

Boy does he have the gift of the gab, I thought.

As we slowly worked our way into the pub, the music got louder, laughter got louder, and the place was swinging.

We had to pay an entry fee, to which Lionel said, 'We've been ripped off $20 ahead.' We were escorted to a table, which sat about 10 people. There were lots of tables and Lionel tried to calculate the dollars collected by table numbers – but we could not accurately count the number of tables. 'Let's say at least 100,' spurted out Lionel, 'That's 100 x 200 per table, that's $20,000? That's a lot of money,' he spurted out.

With a big stage, live music band, various people were singing and acting out their part of karaoke on a big screen, which was hanging off a wall. It was hilariously funny, with a mixture of good singers, very bad singers, sober and drunk singers. There was a cash prize of $1000 for the best performance, based on applause after each participant, and a vote by hands at end of session. No wonder it was popular. As we all sat there, Lucky Phil pulled up a seat next to a girl. Of course, she was not very interested in Phil. I guess she could tell he was a bit pissed. Joe sang along with the others at the table, in bad tune with the karaoke singers. Lionel was tapping on the table with his hand. I was just lying back in my chair, taking it all in.

What a fantastic feeling. So many people were having such great fun, really enjoying themselves. I noticed a guide to the night's events on the table and started to read it. There were different types of themes: rock and roll, groups of various types, 'any classical out there', or 'swingers' and, at the end, 'freestyle' – 'dancing', 'jokes', anything, it said.

It got me thinking, for $1000, could we do something? Maybe to music? With us full of alcohol, I doubted it.

I asked Joe, but he burst out laughing, so much so that everybody started looking at him. This gave me another idea – comedy. I turned to Lionel, and told him my thoughts.

Because I had told Lionel, only, within our group, about my visit to Dr. Wize, regarding the H.1 and H.2 theory. I was wondering if we could do something funny with this. He said, 'As I often do'.

'What do you mean? Well, let's make a skit – a comedy. A couple of lines about H.1 and H.2.'

'You're joking,' he said.

'I'll try to write down some lines we can work on,' was my response. Easier said than done; first I need a pen and paper, I thought. I went and put our names down at reception, to go into the 'freestyle' entertainment section. Luckily, I asked if I could borrow a pen and some paper to write down lines. The reception lady was very helpful and wished me luck.

'I'll need it,' I replied. She laughed out loud. As we sat back at the table, the boys were right into the mood of singing and cheering on the entertainers. I started to write down some lines and told Lionel, 'Let's give it a go.'

'Bullshit,' he spurted out.

'I've already put our names down on list,' I told him. (Was he pissed off!) I said, 'Come on, have a go. It might be good for a laugh.'

'Not me,' he said.

As we sat there, I started to write down some of my thoughts:

H.1, H.2 – which is better for you?
Up high or down low, how far will you go.
Need more or less, no time to confess, show me how now,
H.1, back off, H.2, to go through, H.1 stay cool.
H.2 drool, so hip to lay down, but do not frown.
Be king or queen, and try not to be seen,
Love one another, including your brother,
Do not tease, try to please, do not squeeze, but try to sneeze.
H.1 be happy, H.2 be snappy, H.1 be king, H.2 behave.
H.1 say who, H.2 say thank you, H.1 say goodnight, H.2 do not get a fright.

Sounded good to me. After much discussion between Lionel and I, it was decided the audience would not understand our skit due to them not knowing about H.1 and H.2. They would be confused by it. As I read out the lines to Lionel during a break in music, others at the table thought we were mad, nuts – lost the plot. So, I decided to withdraw our names from the list of entertainers.

At the end of the night, a couple – man and lady – won the $1000 with a comedy about life on the beach. It was very funny.

We eventually found our way back to the apartment. No girls, but we were very happy with the night's entertainment.

The next morning, it was time to go to the beach. With everyone not feeling 100%, we decided to go for a swim before breakfast. 'It might make us feel better,' Phil spurted out.

We nearly drowned. We got pulled out into the ocean by what's called a 'rip', so I was told later. I was swimming forwards, but going further out, it was very strange. I was on the edge of the flags on the beach to show the designated areas to swim in – my error here. I slowly realised the best way back in was to bodysurf the big waves across to within the flagged area, as I was getting worn out trying to swim faster. Luckily for me, this worked as I started getting closer to the beach.

Sand at last. I needed a rest.

I noticed Lucky Phil was busy chatting to a bunch of beautiful girls. Normal for Phil, I thought. With lots of girls sunbaking, cooking themselves, Joe and Lionel drooled over them from a distance. This was our relaxing day. Lucky Phil got on really well with this group of girls, no surprise to us. He came over to the three of us, sitting on the sand, and introduced us to the group of four.

'How lucky are we?'

They were from New South Wales, and it was their first time here also. We all mucked around in the water, sussing one another out. We all seemed to get on okay together.

By late afternoon Lucky Phil asked, 'Have you girls been to the karaoke pub?'

'No,' was their answer.

'Would you all like to go tonight?' he spurted out.

'How good is he to suggest this?' I thought.

'Sounds great,' they said, and all the girls got excited as we told them about our experience there the night before. We needed to get there early since it got very busy quickly. We parted after giving them instructions where the pub was. The girls insisted we meet them there.

'Let's say about 8:00 PM.'

We agreed. All us boys were now fired up to go out with these girls – good natured, happy, fun-loving types. Where would this go? we wondered, as our minds tried to work out who suits who when it came to the seating arrangement.

When we met up with the girls, they all looked drop dead gorgeous. Lucky Phil had it all worked out regarding seating arrangements, but the girls had other ideas. They wanted to sit together. That was okay with Lucky Phil as he sat down next to Barbara, 'the biggest breasted' girl in the group. Lucky Phil's favourite. And with Joe next to Janet, his favourite, Lionel and I were between Lucky Phil and Joe. This did not stop us from having a great night –singing along again, dancing and generally having a ball.

Phil kept making us all laugh with his comments on the 'entertainment'. Boy, his laugh was quite infectious. As the end of the night was fast approaching, we were all a bit tipsy to say the least. Lucky Phil spurted out, 'Let's all go back to our apartment.'

Great idea. All the boys were excited by this, but the girls now let us in on a surprise. Barbara, Phil's favourite said, 'Boys, we would love to go back with you all—' there were smiles from ear to ear on all of us '—but it's not like that. Our parents are up here with us, and they said we could only go out tonight if they pick us up at the end.'

Boy, did the smiles disappear fast. 'No way,' Phil burst out. 'You're kidding us, right?'

'No, they will be out the front waiting for us in about half an hour.'

Lucky Phil asked Barbara, 'Let's dance?' They quickly got up on the dance floor, and, with us watching, Lucky Phil was now all over her. Not a good look from where we were. We could imagine Lucky Phil putting pressure on Barbara for a 'deeper' friendship.

The mood changed at the table when Lucky Phil and Barbara returned. Lucky Phil and Barbara must have had some disagreement on the dance floor – that was my guess. Maybe a knock back on Lucky Phil's advances?

Next thing, Barbara checked her watch, and piped out a, 'Time to go, girls.'

As they walked away, two waving, two blowing air kisses, Lucky Phil skulled a pot of beer and spurted out, 'Let's get really pissed.'

Not far to go, I thought, and the boys all laughed. 'Let's all go back to the apartment,' was my suggestion.

'Alone,' spat Phil. 'No way.'

'Well, you know where we are. See you later,' I said as we all walked out. We did not see Phil that night.

Lucky Phil fronted up the next morning as we were having a coffee, going on about picking up a chick after we left and going back to her place. He then gave us all the details, which we'd all heard before.

Due to this being our last night available at this apartment, and our money disappearing fast, we all decided that this would be our last night here at Coolangatta. After much debate, Lucky Phil insisted we go to Surfer's Paradise; the centre of the Gold Coast. Then he said, 'We might see Bob, Mandy or Teresa there.'

Those names got us all excited, and we agreed to stay one more night only before heading back home. So, to fill in the day, we decided to head to the beach for some 'eye candy' as Phil put it. 'It's the cheapest way to pass time,' he also spurted out.

Boy, was there lots to see. Lucky Phil was in heaven, as we, again, watched him just walk up to a girl or group of girls and introduce himself. In no time at all, he had them laughing. The three of us would just watch him in amazement; was it his accent, tall build, happy nature, the way he walked, talked? We decided it was probably all of these things.

A couple of times, he would gesture to come over and join in. All we could do was listen and laugh. It was difficult to get in any conversation going without interrupting Lucky Phil's hold on attention. On one of these occasions with three girls were all sunbaking, Lucky Phil called us over an introduced us to them. Joe, Lionel, Art – meet Gloria, Sandra, Rose.

After a short time, Lucky Phil and Gloria decided to go for a swim. Into the water they went, rolling around in the waves, so closely wrapped around one another, I could not get the thought out of my mind as to what was going on under the water. Knowing Lucky Phil, I decided to stop staring at them.

My attention was drawn to one of the other girls, Rose. She was just sitting there, not saying anything, looking into the water. Joe, Lionel and Sandra were just lying on the beach – 'getting cooked' I call it.

I asked Rose, 'Do you live local?'

'No,' was her sharp reply – her not wanting to take the conversation much further, I thought.

Then I said her friend in the water seemed to be enjoying herself. (I was trying to get her to lighten up a bit.)

'She's always enjoying herself,' was her sharp reply again.

'Isn't that what we are here for?' I threw back at her.

'Maybe,' was her response.

'Well, what makes you happy?' I asked.

She looked at me in a strange way, and said, 'Why should you care?'

H.1 was now thinking, what would Lucky Phil say now?

I'll hit her with this, came to mind, as I looked her squarely in the eyes.

'A good-looking girl like you should not be looking so sad.' A small smile came to her face, and straight away I said, 'That looks better. Your face sparkles when you smile.' This made her laugh. 'That's better,' I said, 'Sparkles.'

'You're joking,' she spurted out.

'Not to me,' was my response. 'Now that you've laughed, I can see a really good looking side of you.'

'Let's go for a walk,' was her response. We walked along the beach, talking first about lots of interesting spots to see around Coolangatta, then about more personal things.

I asked where she lived. 'Melbourne,' she spurted out.

'No way,' I said, 'I live in Melbourne too.'

As it turned out, she lived in Kew – one of those top suburbs, and she went to one of those ladies-only schools. I straight away wondered if she knew Marilyn from the pool, but I dared not ask her. We walked and talked for hours; she was a very interesting person. Her friends talked her into going to the beach. She said, she was not a beach person, and didn't like sand getting into everything. I straightaway thought, 'I won't go into that scenario.' Lucky Phil would go all out on her with that line.

We made our way back to her friends. As soon as they saw us coming on the beach, her two friends were so worried about her that they ran up and hugged her. 'We thought you got lost,' they spurted out. Lucky Phil straight away spurted out, 'I told you she would be okay with Art.'

'Easy for you to say,' was Gloria's sharp remark.

'Are you okay, Rose?' Sandra asked.

'We just went for a walk.'

'That's all?'

Phil gave me a thumbs up, with his other arm now around Gloria's shoulders, all smiles.

I thought this was going further now. Then Sandra piped up, 'We should be going home now.'

'It's still early,' Lucky Phil spurted out.

Gloria and Rose could see Sandra was a bit upset. 'We'd better go. How about we meet up later?'

Lucky Phil spurted out, 'Where?'

I suggested the karaoke pub. The girls seemed to like this idea. So, we parted, agreeing to meet up later at about 7:30. They knew where the pub was, and said, 'We'll see you later.'

Lucky Phil was so excited. He said Gloria reminded him of Mandy. I knew straight away what he was on about. Joe said he liked Sandra, but did not get on very well. She seemed a bit of a 'toff'.

'I enjoyed Rose's company,' I spurted out.

'What?'

'Did you go back to the apartment?' Lucky Phil spurted out, Joe and Lionel now looking at me with intense eyes.

It would have been so easy to say 'yes' and lead them on, but I could not. Lucky Phil would have said yes to a question like this for sure, I thought. I told them we only walked and talked.

'You're joking,' spurted out Lucky Phil.

'Believe what you want to,' was my response. As we headed back to our apartment, Lucky Phil seemed to be on a natural high due to meeting Gloria. He said they might leave the karaoke early and go back to the apartment. We all knew what that meant.

Joe spurted out that we might be lucky third time around at the karaoke pub. Lionel said he was so burnt and sore, to the point that 'he might stay at the apartment'.

'No way,' spurted out Lucky Phil. 'You are going out with us.'

'Alright,' Lionel quietly said.

Come time to go to the pub, we all showered and cleaned up. We arrived, joined the queue to get in and waited for the girls to turn up. It was nearly 7:45 as we were about to enter the reception and pay to be part of the pub.

I got this feeling that they weren't coming, and said to Lucky Phil, 'No show, mate.'

'Gloria will come soon, I'm sure.'

'The place is nearly full.'

'Are we going in now?' Joe spurted out.

'We'll get a table and seats for girls,' was Lucky Phil's response.

'We will have to pay for them to reserve seats,' spurted Lionel.

'I'll pay,' spurted out Lucky Phil.

'Another $60.'

'You're joking,' said Joe. (I'll pay $20 if Rose turns up, I thought.)

'I'll go halves,' I spurted out.

'Thanks mate', was Lucky Phil's response.

As we settled down at the table, now around 8:30, we all knew. No show girls.

With Lucky Phil's tension building, as he downed his beers faster than asked, he jumped up and yelled out if any Sheilas here wanted to dance. Oh no, I thought. He'd lost it.

'Calm down, mate', I said, as a lot of people turned around to see the commotion going on at our table (no takers, of course). 'Sit down. Tomorrow we will go to the Gold Coast, find Mandy and Teresa,' was all I could think of.

This seemed to calm him down. 'I'm going back to the apartment,' Lionel spurted out.

Joe and I looked at one another. 'Let's take Lucky Phil back also. He's not looking too good now.' Especially after losing count of how many beers he'd had.

'I'm OK,' he drooled. 'Gloria is coming soon.'

'Not now, mate,' was my response.

'Just a bit longer,' Lucky Phil mumbled.

'Only if you stop drinking.'

'Okay mate,' he spurted out.

'We'll wait another half an hour and that's it.'

'Okay mate,' he spurted out again.

Joe and Lionel went for a walk. 'Watch him,' Joe spurted out as he walked off.

'I'll meet you outside soon,' was my response.

After a short while, Lucky Phil started to nod off. I said we should go home now, knowing if he passed out or went to sleep, we were in trouble either way. Just in time, Joe and Lionel came back. Let's go, they said, as we helped Lucky Phil to his feet. We finally made it back to the apartment, and put Phil to bed.

'Where's Gloria?' he spurted out. (Boy, was he taken in by her.)

Joe spat, 'You'll see her tomorrow, mate.'

The next morning, Joe, Lionel and I were all fired up ready to go to the 'real' Gold Coast. We woke Phil up. 'I feel like shit' he spurted out.

'I wonder why' Lionel said. We all laughed.

'Not funny,' Phil said, as he held his hand as if it was going to full off his shoulder. 'What happened?' he spurted out.

'Not much.'

'Thanks to you,' said Joe.

'No show by the girls. You got really pissed,' said Lionel.

'I can't remember too much,' Phil spurted out.

'Just as well,' I said.

'Get cleaned up. We have to get out of here; it's nearly 10 and we should be gone from here. Hand the keys back so we will get out deposit money back,' Lionel spurted out.

'Okay mate,' was all Phil could manage to say. 'I'll go get the car and load up. Give me the keys. I'll sort things out downstairs, get our deposit back.'

'That's all I have to spend,' Joe spurts out.

'I'm not far from broke,' Lionel said. 'Don't look at me.'

'I've only got about $200 left. Don't count on Lucky Phil, he's probably lost his wallet.'

'Speaking from experience,' Joe spurted out.

'Okay, let's just get going up to the Gold Coast,' Lionel spurted out.

'Well, we've come this far. It's only another couple of hours, might as well have a look,' was my response.

It didn't seem to take that long until we were driving along the main beach of the Gold Coast. Lucky Phil, now feeling a bit better, said, 'I hope we bump into Bob today.'

We all laughed at this thought, and I said, 'What about Mandy, Teresa or Gloria?' Joe, Lionel and me were now all laughing hysterically.

'Not funny,' spurted out Phil. 'I need a drink.'

'Got my money?' Lionel spat out.

'Of course,' Phil spurts out, as he pulled out his wallet and opened it up. 'Shit,' was his response. 'Where's my money gone? I had hundreds in here.'

'When was that?' Joe spurted out.

'A couple of days ago, I guess.'

'Yeah, well, you probably spent 100 or more last night.'

'You're joking,' said Phil.

'Don't you remember buying tickets for the girls' seats, and them not turning up?'

'Oh yeah.'

'And then all those beers you bought.'

'Oh yeah.'

Then Phil asked if we could lend him $50.

'We're all a bit short,' piped up Lionel.

What now then? We all looked at one another. 'Never thought about running out of money, boys,' was my response.

As none of us had a bank book or any other way to get money, what could we do?

Being a Friday, about lunch time, I decide to ring Mum. We were so lucky to have a telephone installed at home (Mum and Dad had, just a few months earlier, got the phone put in. Mum had, for ages, wanted a phone. We sometimes used our neighbours' phone, and paid them for a phone call, until Dad finally got Mum one.)

When I rang Mum, she was so excited to hear from me. (I had forgotten to ring her when we arrived in Queensland like I said I would, so she could be not happy for not ringing her then.) She was so worried, but understood about my forgetfulness, due to having such a good time with the boys, and being on the beach.

When I explained how we were all nearly out of money, and needed some today, she could not believe it.

'It goes too fast up here, Mum. Everything is so expensive,' was all I could think of. I told her I inquired at the post office up here and they told me that you could take money to the post office down at the mall, and they could transfer it up to here.

'Down to the mall!' she spurted out. 'How much?' was her next question.

'$100.'

'How much?' she yelled out.

'I'll pay you back when I get home. We need petrol money to get home,' was all I could think of. (Which I hadn't really thought of until now.)

'We don't have much more than that in the bank,' Mum spurted out.

'I have more than that in my bank. I'll pay you back on Monday – we will be back home on Monday.'

'But Dad's at work, I'll have to catch the bus to the mall, go to the bank, go to the post office.'

'I'm sorry, Mum, but we must have this money today to come home by Monday.'

'What do I need to do?'

I explained to Mum how to transfer her money into the mall post office and they would transfer it up to the Gold Coast post office.

'That's all going to take a while,' she spurted out, 'a couple of hours, I guess,' she said.

'I know, Mum. We don't have any other choice.'

'Okay, I'll go now.'

'Thanks Mum.'

'I love you lots. Kisses over the phone.' (Still not happy.) 'See you Monday. You look after yourself,' were mum's parting words.

This seemed to have solved one of our problems, money, but we still needed to find a place to stay a couple of nights after my phone call to Mum. The boys were keen to look around. This place was so big, with all these high-rise buildings.

'Must be plenty of places to stay,' said Lionel. 'We'd better find a place to stay first.'

After lots of asking at various high-rise apartments (it was even more expensive than Coolangatta), we finally found a backpacker pub with a room for four people (two bunk beds that reminded me of our bungalow). They were very small rooms, very cheap.

'Good,' said the boys.

'I can only give you two nights.'

'Perfect.' Lucky Phil was keen to do a pub crawl, trying to find Bob, Mandy and Teresa, and Gloria.

'We should all stick together here or we will get lost,' Lionel spurted out.

'Let's get food,' was Joe's answer. 'Lots of cafes to choose from,' he also spurted out.

'Counter lunch, overlooking the beaches,' was Lucky Phil's response.

'Anything will do me,' I spat out.

With the beach on one side of the main road, and pubs on the opposite side, Lucky Phil yelled out, 'This one looks good.'

With a great view over the beach, it was also the closest one to the beach, as he pointed out. We ordered up food and drinks. 'Look at all these beautiful babes,' Phil spurted out as a couple of girls walked past, within reach of Phil's loud voice.

They turned and smiled, 'Lucky Phil's feeling better,' I spurted out and we all started laughing. Lucky Phil could not take his eyes off all the people passing us in the street. We were sitting at a table right next to the footpath. Even while eating, drinking, talking, and commenting on passers-by, his eyes never stopped looking around. Like he was in another world, I thought.

Joe piped up and said, 'If you need to go for a piss, I'll watch everyone for you.' And we all cracked up laughing. Even Phil could see the funny side of this, and his laugh smothered ours, to a point where, he got a tap on the shoulder and he turned around.

'Bob, is that you under those whiskers?'

Now looking a bit rough for wear, Bob spurted out 'I knew that laugh straight away. I was over there playing pool. How's it going boys?' was his first question. And before we could answer, 'Can I give you anything, Lucky Phil?'

'How's the smokes going?'

'Not much left,' was his reply, 'due to supply and demand', he added with a wink. 'I need ten dollars each.'

'Each!' Lucky Phil yelled out.

'Not so loud, mate.'

'Not so dear, mate,' said Phil.

'Well, for you, eight dollars.'

Joe piped up, 'We don't have much money left, mate.'

'Everybody has that problem,' was Bob's answer. All went quiet.

'I'll think about it,' Phil spurted out, with a shocked look on his face.

'I'll be over there, but for only a little while,' he said as he walked away.

'I bet you wished that tap on the shoulder was Mandy,' Joe spurted out, and we all crack up laughing – all except Phil.

'See, you don't need Bob to make us laugh,' I spurted out, and Lucky Phil started to see the funny side as to what just happened.

'Let's just have a nice relaxing time here, watching the babes, dreaming of Mandy, Teresa and Gloria. Rose, if you want to, Art,' piped up Joe.

Lionel pointed out a beautiful blonde. 'She looks a bit like Rose, Art, don't you think?'

I laughed and said Rose had bigger boobs, and we all cracked up laughing.

'What about that brunette over there? She looks a bit like Gloria.'

'I wish,' said Lucky Phil, starting to laugh out loud again.

'Wait for that tap on the shoulder again,' I said, and we all could not stop laughing, even Lionel, bent over with stomach cramps from laughing so much.

As we sat there, slowly sipping our beers, reminiscing on the last few days, looking at all the people on the street and beach, hundreds of them, we wondered how many other people have had such experiences as us. We realised how lucky we were just to be here.

All of a sudden, I realised it was 4:45 p.m. 'Shit. The post office will be closing at 5.' I jumped up and started running. 'I'll be back ASAP.' And I took off. It was blocks away, but I ran flat out, knowing I must get this money today or we would be in really deep shit with no money.

After what seemed like ages, but was only 10 minutes, I arrived at the post office with five minutes to spare – but there was a queue at the counter with about 10 – 12 people in front of me. As I watched the big clock over the counter ticking closer to 5:00, I started to panic, thinking, will I make it in time? At that moment, a man walked out behind the counter and closed the doors behind me. I looked at him as if to say 'am I going to be served?' He could see my look and said, 'You're our last customer.'

Boy, was I relieved. Then, as I got closer to the counter, I got a horrible feeling. What if something went wrong with Mum getting the money and transferring it up to here? I started to panic and feel a bit sick. I knew Mum sort of understood, but she had a lot to do; catch the bus to the mall, get money from the bank, go to the post office, transfer to here, what could go wrong? I felt like I was starting to go white with fright. I was thinking, if it's not here, what would we do?

As I got to the counter, the nice and polite lady said, 'Are you okay, son? You don't look so good.'

'It all depends,' I said. 'My name is Arthur, and my mum has transferred some money to here from Melbourne.'

She smiled and said, 'This happens all the time here. Do you have your ID – a driver's licence or something?'

I hadn't even thought about this, but boy, I could not get my licence out of my wallet quick enough.

'Okay, let's have a look at what's here,' she said, as she slowly flipped through a pile of papers on the counter behind her. My heart was racing so much, I could feel my temperature rising, to a point I'm sure was above normal. As she got closer to the bottom of the pile, peeling back page after page, I thought, oh no, it's not there. It must've been at the second or third last page when she finally said, 'Arthur, here it is.'

My heart almost stopped. 'One hundred dollars,' she said. 'That's a lot of money. You must have a very good mum.' She laughed.

'The best', I said, and she counted out the money.

'Have a good weekend.' It was her last words.

'I will now.' She laughed again. As she opened the door to let me out, a man older than me was trying to get in.

'Sorry we are closed,' was her response.

'But I need –'

'Sorry we are closed,' she said, and she shut the door.

As I walked away, I could not help but feel for the man outside the door. That could have been me, five minutes late, again – how lucky was I?

When I arrived back with the boys, 'Surprise, surprise'. Lucky Phil, laughed, I could hear him from down the footpath as I approached. There were two drop dead gorgeous girls sitting with them.

'Art!' Lucky Phil yelled out. 'Meet Simone and Terry.' Joe and Lionel were all smiles. 'We have been invited to a party tonight, up on one of those high-rise apartments. Simone says the view is fantastic and we are all invited!'

Terry said, 'We will have some friends coming over tonight. I hope you'll come, Arthur.' She spurted out in a laughing manner, a bit like Lucky Phil's manner – joking around, I thought.

'Sounds great to me. What's the occasion?' I responded.

'To celebrate new friends.'

'I've never heard of a party like this before,' was all I could think of. Everybody cracks up laughing. 'Has Bob been around?' I asked Lionel.

'No,' he spurted out, with Lucky Phil and Joe now bending over laughing with stomach pains. (The girls were also laughing.) I noticed the ashtray on the table was full of butts, very small butts, like the type Bob had with no filters on them, and then I got a whiff of this smell from them, and I knew straight away what was going on. I looked at Lionel, and said 'Did you have one of those?' and pointed to the ashtray.

'No,' he spurted out.

'Only half,' added Joe.

As everybody was now laughing so much, people around started looking at us as if to say, 'What's going on over there'. It turns out the girls offered the boys a smoke each.

Lucky Phil explained how he met Simone and Terry at the bar and offered them a drink, and now in return, they offered us to a party tonight. Everybody was laughing so much now, I automatically joined in.

As the sun started to go down, Simone said, 'See you boys around eight o'clock then,' and handed Lucky Phil a piece of paper. 'This is where we are – bring a couple of drinks, boys,'

Terry yelled out, as they walked away.

Lucky Phil, Joe, Lionel and I were all now so excited. We were going to a party, and 'We have the address!' Lucky Phil spurts out.

'Thanks to you, Phil!' Lionel spurted out. Lionel seemed to be more excited than normal – it was probably that 'half' smoke he had, I thought.

As we all headed back to the backpacker's pub – people everywhere, chockers, full to the brim – we find our way to our one room with two bunk beds.

'I want the top one,' Joe yells out.

'Me too,' says Lionel.

'I'm easy. Looks like it's you and me on bottom bunks.'

'Good,' Phil spurted out. 'I don't like it on top.'

'That's not what I've heard,' Joe yelled out. Everybody started laughing at his comment, knowing its double meaning.

'This is fantastic,' Lionel spurted out, as he tried to find his cleanest clothes to go to the party in. Each of us with only minimal clothes in small bags, started going through them.

'Does this look clean to you, Art?' Joe asked, with very little light in the room. It was his old t-shirt.

'On its last legs, but looks okay to me.'

'Hey Lionel, you smell a bit funny to me,' Joe gestures to me to stir up Lionel by moving both his arms in a circular motion.

'I've got some aftershave spray on – you can have some,' was my response. As Lionel doused himself with it everywhere, Phil yelled out, 'Save some for me!' and we all burst out laughing. Soon we were ready to go, all washed up, smelling good.

'Maybe the clothes could do with a wash,' Lionel spurted out.

'Just give them a spray with that aftershave.'

'If there's any left,' Phil spurted out. Lucky Phil suggested we buy some of those 'girly drinks'. 'You know, those coloured ones.'

'Sounds expensive,' said Lionel.

'Let's have a look at the bottle shop around the corner,' Phil says.

'We'll get a mixture,' Joe said, as we walked into the shop.

'Can I help you boys?' said the man serving.

'Yes,' spurted out Phil. 'We're going to a party and want some colourful drinks for the girls, and a couple for us.'

'Okay, let's see.'

'Not too dear!' Lionel yelled out to the attendant.

'These cans are popular with the girls,' he said. 'Vodka, gin. Southern Comfort. Already mixed.'

'Sounds good. Give us a mixture and throw in some beers – cans, cold ones,' was Phil's instructions.

We ended up with a big box full of cans. Luckily the high-rise apartment wasn't that far away. After getting instructions from our friendly bottle shop man, we headed off talking about the night ahead.

Lucky Phil spurted out, 'Simone is mine, boys. Lay off her.'

'I like Terry,' Lionel jumped in.

Joe said he will wait to see.

'I'm easy,' was all I could think of.

'We all knew that,' Phil spurted out, and everybody cracked up laughing again at Phil's laugh. We soon arrived at the address.

'Shit. This is a high, high, apartment block,' Lucky Phil yelled out.

'What number unit are we looking for?' Joe piped up.

'20A,' Phil yelled out as we walked up to the big doors at the big entrance.

'It's locked,' yelled out Lionel.

'It can't be,' said Joe.

Lucky Phil had seen this type of door before and said, 'I think you have to push a button, over there, on the wall where all those numbers are. Here's 20A – well, push it, Joe!' Lucky Phil fumbled with the big box of cans on his shoulder. 'Is that you Simone?' Phil said to a voice coming from a speaker in the wall.

'Yes, I'll open the door for you, boys,' was her answer. 'Just push it now.' We heard a clicking noise within the door, *click* and it opened. Amazing, I thought.

As we went into the foyer, Joe noted, 'This is one hell of a top spot'. 'Look at the marble on the floor, look at that finish on the walls, look at that over there, the trimmings – is that gold or brass? Very shiny.'

The lift door opened, and two men in suits step out – they both immediately eye us up and down, as if they had never seen a group of boys before, or maybe because Phil had the big box of cans on his shoulder, wearing the biggest smile.

'G'day,' Phil spurted out to them; silence was their response.

The doors closed and we all went up 20th floor, all of us wondering, 'what next'

Lionel said, 'I wonder how many girls will be at this party.'

Lucky Phil spurted out, 'Lots, I hope.'

Lionel reinforced the point that he really likes Terry, and Joe spurted out that he did too.

'Boys,' said Phil, 'Simone's mine, don't forget.'

The door opened on the 20th floor and just as Lucky Phil stepped out of the lift, he quickly took a step back. 'Shit', he spurted out, as he looked to the window next to the lift. 'We are up too high for me.'

'He hates heights,' Joe spurted out.

Too late now, was my thought. 'It's okay mate.'

We might get higher later,' Joe laughed out loud.

Lucky Phil spurted out, 'Not funny', and groaned, looking away from the window. 'There's 20A at the other end of the lifts.'

As we walked towards 20A, there was another window next to the door. Lucky Phil backed off.

'Look at that fantastic view of the beach – the lights, the buildings,' I spurted out, trying to brighten things up. Lucky Phil was not impressed at all.

Joe knocked on the door, and it opened straight away. Simone, looking absolutely stunning, was looking at three of us standing in doorway, and straight away said, 'Where's Phil?'

'Over here,' he yelled out. Simone sighed with relief.

'Phil hates heights,' spurted out Joe, with Phil standing beside the window, not looking out. Simone brushed past us to grab Phil by the arm, and pulled him into the doorway, past the window, nearly dropping the big box of cans still on his shoulder.

'Put that down on this bench,' Simone said, as we all followed her into the apartment. With soft music playing, Terry came into the main room. (This main room with a lounge, dining and kitchen was very big compared to our Coolangatta apartment, I thought.) Terry also looked drop dead gorgeous.

'HI boys,' she calmly said. 'What would you all like to drink?' she asked as she pointed to a bar area in the corner of the room, next to the big balcony doors with blinds pulled three quarters of the way down (lucky for Phil, I thought).

'We've got drinks for all of us,' Joe spurted out as he went and grabbed the big box of cans, taking them to the bar area, and started pulling them out, lining them up on bar top bench next to fridge. Terry seemed impressed, her and Joe all smiles.

Lucky Phil piped up, 'Boy, you girls look fantastic.'

Off to a good start, I thought, but it was true.

As Joe, Lionel and I were looking over the apartment, Joe spurted out, 'This is a great apartment, girls.'

'It's the best,' was Terry's reply.

'Are we too early for the party?' Lionel announced.

'Not at all,' Simone quickly replied. 'Our friends are not far away.' Terry laughed. (I could not see the joke.)

'Let's talk for a while.' We are each handed a coldie by Terry. Simone started talking about their stay here; they only came once a year, and this was their third year (they must be a bit older than us, I thought). Simone seemed to do most of the talking, with a hand on Phil's leg (Phil always smiling). Terry nodded a lot, laughing a lot.

The room had an unusual smell to it, but I liked it. I noticed a couple of candles burning in another corner of the room. Okay, I thought. That's the smell. After a while, and a couple of quick coldies downed, Simone asked us if we 'All want to have a good time tonight?', which seemed an unusual question to me. Lucky Phil's face lit up, and Joe seemed to jump into life and head towards Terry, who was standing now near the balcony doors. Lionel looked a bit dumbfounded by this question, and I must have looked surprised, I guess. Simone said she had four more friends who would 'like to join our party', but they were 'all girls – no other boys coming'. The look on all of our faces must have been priceless, with smiles so big that caused me to crack up laughing.

'You're joking,' said Lucky Phil.

'Do you mind?' spurted out Simone.

'Not at all,' spurted out Phil.

'What about you boys?' she asked as she turned to us, all smiles as we collectively nodded and said 'Great.'

'Do they dance?' asked Joe.

'They sure do,' said Terry. 'I'll give them a ring then, they're not far away.' And again, Terry burst out laughing.

'Next door, actually,' Simone spurted out. She also said that her friends liked to party hard. I thought, 'what does that mean?'

Lucky Phil spurted out, 'How hard?'

Simone looked at Terry and said, 'They do not hold back. Anything goes. That's how our friends' parties go.'

All of us boys were now bursting in anticipation of what was going on, as Phil just shrugged his shoulders.

'We'll just go next door and see if they are ready. You boys help yourself to drinks – won't be long,' Simone said. 'Don't turn up the music, the neighbours might not like it loud.'

Terry also went next door. As the girls closed the door, we all could not believe it.

'We've hit the Jack pot,' Joe yelled out. 'Six girls, four boys. The odds are looking good.'

Straight away Lucky Phil reminded us that Simone is his favourite, and Joe and Lionel, started arguing about Terry. I piped in, 'What about the other four girls?'

All goes quiet. 'Let's wait and see,' Phil spurted out. After about ten minutes, the girls came back into the apartment. All six girls were looking absolutely stunning – all with makeup on, short dresses, smelling amazing and outstanding hairstyles (this was my first thought).

'Girls,' said Simone, 'meet Phil, Joe, Lionel and Art. Boys, this is Jody, Joy, Gail and Bridget.'

'Wow,' we all seem to say together.

'We are all very, very, pleased to meet you,' Phil quickly spurted out.

There were just enough chairs and room on the couch to fit everyone into the lounge area. There were two other doors of this area, I thought. Must be bedrooms. I asked about the toilet, and Simone said either door will lead you to one. Great.

As I entered one of the doors, I noticed a big double bed in the room with an ensuite at the end of it. Toilet inside here, I thought. I went right through. What a great bathroom, spacious, very flash finishes. Job done, I went back to the lounge room. All girls were now drinking and talking (Phil and Simone doing most of that). Joe was up dancing with Judy, Lionel was dancing with Joy. I sat between Gail and Bridget, talking about the beach, with jokes thrown in, and some of Phil's experience with ladies which seemed to get all the girls' attention. It wasn't very long before the hitchhiker, 'Bob' friend was mentioned.

Terry then spurted out, 'Let's get this party swinging. Who would like a smoke?' She opened up her large handbag next to the couch and started handing them out.

As she passed them around, all the girls got one. Then, Phil, Joe, Lionel and me. Phil jumped up straight away and started lighting up each one. When he comes to me, I hesitate and say, 'I'll wait a while mate,' and put the smoke on top of my ear, as I have seen other 'cool' dudes do this.

No one seem to notice me doing this except Phil who gives me a dirty look. I have not seen a look like this from Phil before. He quickly sits back down, now everyone smoking (except me). I suggested to Simone that I open up the blinds to see the view outside.

'Of course,' she replied.

'But what about Phil?' I asked.

'I'll take care of that,' she spurted out.

'Let's all dance,' spurts out Joe, as he helps two girls to their feet.

'Do you rock 'n' roll? he mumbles to them.

'We love rock 'n' roll,' they said as Joe and the girls start dancing. Lionel decides to dance with two girls also, one on each arm swinging and twisting to Elvis, tripping over one another at times, but always laughing. With four girls now dancing, Simone sitting on Phil's lap, kissing him a lot, me on the balcony with Gail.

'Does not get much better than this,' I said to Gail.

'It does,' was her reply. Not knowing what she meant. As we talked out on the balcony taking in the magnificent views, the boys and girls were inside laughing lots (due to the smoke I thought). After a while things inside quietened down and I noticed Lucky Phil and Simone, and Joe and Terry were not in the lounge room.

I asked Gail, 'Have they gone out somewhere?'

She said, 'They are in good hands.' Again, not knowing what she meant. I noticed the balcony was joined onto the next balcony and asked if that was their balcony.

'Yes,' she said, and showed me how you can open up the glass gate between them. As we opened the gates to my surprise the blinds on their bedroom window were up, no lights on. I could see Lucky Phil sitting on top of Simone. What a sight! Gail also saw this and pulled me back (she did not seem as embarrassed as I was) and said we best to go back onto the other balcony. We walked past the balcony doors to the other end of the balcony, again a window into the bedroom of the lounge room, where Lionel and the girls were now sitting down drinking.

'Is that Joe in bed?' I said to Gail.

'That looks like Terry also,' she spurted out. Gail and I both went back inside.

Lionel said to me, 'You look like you just saw a ghost.'

'Sort of,' I said.

The girls were now sitting around the table, smoking, drinking, laughing.

I whispered to Lionel, 'Go out to the balcony, turn left, look into the window.'

'Why Art?'

'Just do it.' He soon came back.

'Shit,' he said, 'Is that Lucky Phil and Simone?'

'Yep,' I replied, 'Now go and turn right.'

'Why?'

'Just do it,' I said again. He came running back.

'Is that Joe and Terry?'

'Must be,' I replied, 'They are not here.'

With the four girls now sitting at the table, Lionel and me on the couch, Gail comes over and takes Lionel by the hand and said, 'Let's go.'

She opened the door into the other bedroom of the lounge room. I was stunned, knowing what was probably going to happen in there. Then Judy comes over to me.

'Let's go next door,' she spurted out as she lifted me up with her hand outstretched. I could not resist her. As we walked out the front door and into her apartment, Lucky Phil and Simone were coming out, Phil all smiles. Simone blows Judy a kiss and said, 'Have fun.'

As soon as the apartment door closes, Judy opened the bedroom door and pipes out, 'Let's do it,' and pushes me onto the bed. We could not get our clothes off quick enough. H.1 thinking "I'm dreaming", H.2 growing so fast.

'Oh no,' I realised, 'No condom.' H.1 was going crazy as I watched Judy remove her bra and undies, her silhouette in the moonlight from the window was amazing. She then opens the side drawer on the bed and takes out a condom, what a relief H.1 straight away thinks, as she rolls it on to me, my heart now racing at twice its normal speed, I'm sure. She pushes me down flat onto the bed and climbs on top, grabbing H.2 as it was going into the wrong place, and slowly inserted H.2 into her. I could not believe what was happening, as she slowly moved up and down on me at first, then faster and faster, it was like she was riding a horse, (I thought – get this out of H.1 now). She grabbed both of my hands and put them on her boobs.

'Hold them, please,' she muttered. They were going crazy, it put a whole new meaning to name of the song 'Shake, Rattle and Roll', which was playing in the lounge room. It was an unbelievable experience.

After a short while, Judy said we should get back to the lounge room.

'I'm in no hurry,' I spurted out, as she climbed out of bed and put her clothes back on. So quickly, I thought to myself. When I came back into the lounge room, now with Joe and Joy missing, (me thinking where are they?) and Phil sitting on the couch with Terry all over him, sitting on his knees like Simone was, and kissing him on his chest, now no t-shirt on. Simone comes up to me and suggests that we go onto the balcony.

'Take in the view,' she said.

'Sounds good to me' I spurted out. As we were admiring the magnificent view, over the ocean and the lights below, I said to Simone, 'Everything seems to be moving so slowly'. And with only me and Simone on the balcony, to my surprise she starts to talk softly about her friends.

'Do you like my friends?' she asks.

'Yes, a lot. They are so friendly,' was my response.

'Great', she said, and went on to say how as friends they share everything. 'I mean everything. Take this party for example, Phil and I have just shared something special.' ('I know' H.1 thought straight away). 'We just made love together' she said softly. 'You don't look surprised?' she spurted out.

I replied, 'I put one and one together,' and came up with, 'That's what Lucky Phil was on about when he said, "I've just had the best time of my life"'.

'How would you like to have the same feeling?' Simone spurts out with a big smile.

'But what about Phil?' Was my response. Simone's response also shocked me.

'Look at him now on the couch with Terry on his lap. He won't be there much longer.'

'He's happy by the look of it'.

Simone takes me by the hand and we slowly walked past everyone, them laughing, some dancing, straight into a bedroom. As we entered the bedroom and Simone closed the door, all I could see were a couple of candles flickering around the big bed, straightaway I thought H.1 control H.2. What next?

Before I could even think with H.1, Simone pushed me onto the bed and straight away removed her top to reveal the best pair of boobs I had ever seen. With the candle lights flickering, I could see her large nipples. H.2 fired up as she removed my shirt, and H.1 started to go wild as she dropped her skirt and undies together. It was all happening so fast, too many thoughts running through H.1 as Simone then undid my belt and slowly pulled down my shorts, H.2 now popping out of my jocks.

'Wow', Simone says, 'That looks good. No foreskin. I have something for that,' as she removes my jocks to fully expose H.2. As she leaned over to open the bedside table drawer, I could not believe it, another condom. 'You should use this.'

'I could not agree more,' I said, 'I was going to ask you about something like that' and she laughed.

'Don't you worry, we are going to be fine,' and she rolled it onto H.2. Then she positioned herself on to me, flat out on the bed, suggesting, 'Let's roll over,' and with a gentle push to the side, I was on top, deep inside her, H.2 about to explode. 'Wait', she said as she rolled up back over, her on top again as H.2 explodes, she leans back as if to try and snap H.2 off. I rose up with her and pulled her into me, her breasts squished against my chest. She grunts 'That was fantastic.'

'For me too,' was the only reply I could think of.

She then leaned forward and kind of slapped my face with her boobs side to side. This I had never experienced either, and then said to 'suck them'. It felt so good. She said to lick them and she became very wet, 'like Virginia', I thought. We both just laid there all gasping for air. What another experience, H.1 thought. Simone started kissing me, thanking me.

'We better go back to the lounge room,' she said. Except I wanted to stay there forever with her. As she quickly got dressed and blew me a kiss on her way out, she then went on to say, 'All my friends are very close' and if I would mind if they share the same experience with them.

'Not at all,' I spurted out straight away.

'I'll be back soon,' Simone said.

Within a minute, Bridget opened the door, the shortest and youngest. She seemed both shy and quiet and said, 'I'll go to the bathroom first.'

Within a minute she opens the ensuite door, the light on and standing sideways, her naked body was shining in the light. Her boobs are so pointed, I noticed. She slowly walked over and opened the draw to take out another condom. 'How many of them are in there?' H.1 thinks. This thought soon disappeared as she slid into the bed next to me, feeling H.2 straight up.

'It's starting to grow again,' I said. She laughs as she removes the condom from its wrapper. H.2 high again. How can this be the third time tonight? Except, H.2 isn't as high as it was with Simone, I thought. Until Bridget asked made to roll on top of her and then said, 'Let me roll it onto you,' as I kneeled up H.2. It is almost at its max now, I thought. As I penetrated Bridget, she let out a bit of a sigh.

'Are you okay?' I asked.

'It feels great,' she replied, as we both started moving, faster and faster together, it seemed like we were stuck to one another. Then she became all wet and I knew what had happened as she let out a big sigh.

'Thank you,' she said, as I collapsed onto her.

'Am I squashing you?' I spurted out.

'Squash me all you like.' She spurted out as I started kissing her breasts, so hard but so soft at the same time, I thought. We were both now trying to separate and as H.2 pulls out, the condom comes off. I could feel this and I grabbed it just in time, to fully remove it, from Bridget.

'That was close!' I spurted out, as Bridget realised what had just happened.

Bridget then says that Joy and Gail would like to come in, but I said 'I need a drink' first, as we both got dressed and went back into the lounge. Only Lionel was there on his own, asleep on the couch. Joe, Phil, Simone, Joy, Gail and Terry were not there either, only Bridget, me and Lionel.

Bridget said, 'I'll get you a drink, they will probably be back soon'. After what seemed like ages, I knocked off the coldie and Bridget also had a drink, talking about how Lionel could go to sleep. I told her he has had a big day from this morning, this afternoon, and now, he has drunk too much, probably smoked too much.

'He's ratshit,' I spurted out. Next thing, everybody came in from next door unit, all smiling, Phil laughing as usual.

'How's it hanging?' Phill spurted out, knowing what's been going on.

'I need a break,' I said, all the girls now laughing so much.

Simone said, 'Are you having a good time?'

'The best of my life,' I spurted out.

'Me too,' spurted out Phil and Joe.

'Lionel's bombed it,' I said. 'How unlucky is he now.' As it was now very late, (mid-morning, I'm guessing), the girls said that it was time to go to bed.

'Again!' spurted out Phil.

'You come with me,' yelled out Judy.

'Joe, you're with me,' Gail yelled out.

Terry then grabs my hand and said, 'You're coming with me'.

So off we go into her bedroom, leaving Lionel, Simone, Joy and Bridget to sort things out. Well, wasn't Terry keen to get into bed. I was still undressing when she was already in bed, opening the draw for you-know-what, with no blankets over her and the candles flickering. She looked fantastic. Can I do it again? (H .1 wonders). Terry saw the look on my face and said we can take it slowly now, as everyone's in bed to stay. Thank god, H.1 thought, and as I got into bed with Terry, she grabbed my hand and put it onto her vagina, myself understanding what this might mean. I started to rub her (no hair here I thought), as she gently pushes my finger into her (I knew what to do). She sighed with relief and started moving my finger up and down. As I did this, I could see her smiling, enjoying my movements, then she grabbed my hand again and said, 'Let me put this on you first, before you have an explosion.'

'Good idea,' I said. Bringing back memories again of Virginia, as she rolled on the condom, H.2 now getting very high, again, I thought, as she again put my hand and finger into her. She wanted it to move faster up and down. I could feel the softest part with each movement, then all of a sudden, she orgasmed, and Terry started shaking all over, pulling my hand away and said 'go', as if now to penetrate her with H.2. As I did this, it seemed so different to the others, very wet and somehow soothing to me. As I soon exploded into her, she whispered more, more; I tried to explode again, but I couldn't. Terry was 'very happy' she said as we separated.

Terry said, 'It's time to sleep now. How good idea was that?'

As we lay there, the door opens, and Joy entered.

'We are going to sleep, now,' Terry yelled out.

'Can I join you?' Joy asked.

'What do you think?' Terry asked me.

'Okay, I guess, but I'm very tired.' Not to mention H.2 was worn out.

Joy said, 'I just want a cuddle,' as she slides in next to me, and as I move over a bit, Terry said goodnight to us both. Within a minute, Joy slid her hand onto H.2 (not very big now), but her hand felt warm as she started squeezing H.2, nothing more, just squeezing, my thought, now touch her. With no undies on, no dress on, only her top on, I could not resist, doing the same to Joy, as with Terry. She started to shake. I felt the orgasm and she sighed. It was all over so quickly, I thought. She removed her hand and rolled over. 'Is that it?' H.1 thought. Within minutes we were all asleep.

In the morning, we all slowly turned up into the lounge room, Lionel up first (I'm guessing). When I woke up, Terry was still asleep, Joy no longer in bed with us. I walked into the lounge, still in a daze, looking around, Lionel holding his head with a coffee in front of him.

'Smells good,' I said to him, 'Anyone else up?'

'Joy and Simone went for a run as I was making myself a coffee.'

Phil and Jody came in. 'What a night,' Phil spurted out, and started his laugh; no one joined in. Then Joe and Gail came out, all smiles, looking worse for wear, I thought.

'Where's everyone else?' Joe spurted out.

'Terry's asleep, so is Bridget,' said Judy.

'Joy and Simone gone for a run,' I said.

'What's for breakfast?' Joe spurted out.

'Whatever you want to go get,' said Lionel. Everybody now sitting down, talking a lot about last night and how good it was for everyone. Terry then comes in with Bridget.

'Where are Simone and Joy?' she asked.

'Out running,' was my answer.

We all sit down, lots of questions about last night, when Simone and Joy come back in, bright as buttons.

Simone says, 'I'm having a shower.'

Straight away, Phil popped up and said, 'I'll help you.' Everybody laughed.

'No, I'll be quicker by myself,' she spurted out. Joy also said that she'll be having a shower too, and Joe yelled out, 'Do need some help!?'

'I'm good also,' she replied, both boys now looking sad. Terry told us we all have to get out of here by 10:00 a.m. - hand keys back, get deposit back, heading home, mid NSW.

Phil jumped in quickly, 'We need phone numbers, addresses.'

Terry jumped in just as quick as Phil and then said to us all, 'All of us girls have an agreement not to get attached to anybody we meet on our holidays. We all agreed not to give any personal information to anybody we meet'. She went on to explain, 'We all want to have a good time and share everything together, experiences and friendships. As I told you yesterday, it all started about three years ago, when Simone and I came here for Christmas. We had a reasonably good time, but had a bad experience with a couple of men. I won't go into that, but we were lucky, it could have been very bad for us. We stayed at a cheap place, and learned a lot by our mistakes.'

Phil jumped in. 'We are not like that,' in a very serious voice.

'I know,' said Terry. 'But our rules are very clear. No more contact,' she spurts out. 'We all live on farms and go to universities. This makes it even more complicated. I have already told you all too much. Simone and I asked Joy and Judy to share costs with us, and Gail and Bridget also wanted to come this year, to share the costs and experiences.'

'We would like to come up next year and share the costs also,' Phil spurted out.

'I don't know if we will come here next year,' was her reply.

'I can give you my phone number,' I spurted out. 'So you can ring me next year, and we can meet up.'

'Not going to happen,' she said. I was disappointed, as was all the other boys, I guess. As Simone and Joy came back into the lounge, Terry said, 'I have just told the boys about our girl rules and agreements.'

'No wonder they look so sad,' Simone spurted out. 'We have to pack up now,' she added, 'It's 9:30.' And she then does something I will never forget. She hands each one of us a piece of paper and a pen. And then tells us to read it carefully.

'It's a survey. As we are all Uni students, this helps us with our studies. Can you boys help us, by answering some questions on the page, please?'

With her big smile, how could we resist? As we all sit around the table, the girls panicking and packing their cases with clothes and shoes, cleaning up a bit.

Then Terry yelled out, 'We are just going to load up the car and book out of here, take our keys back and get our deposit back. We will be back in about 10 to 15 minutes.'

'Okay, sure!' Phil yelled out, as the girls closed the door on the way out.

As I started reading the survey, I glanced across to see the look on Lionel's face, as Joe started coughing and Lucky Phil started laughing. I then noticed the survey had my name on it.

I asked the boys, 'Is your name on the survey?'

'Yes,' was their reply.

I could not believe what I was reading, it was a questionnaire on our experiences with each of the girls. After reading about 10 questions, I asked Lucky Phil, 'What's going on here?'

'Buggered if I know,' he spurted out.

Joe said, 'This is fascinating. Look at Question Number 2, 'Who was the best performer?''

'What about number four?' Lionel spurted out. '''Who gets the highest 'score' out of all the girls, for each 'act' they carried out?'' Did I miss out on something?'

'You sure did,' spurted out Joe. 'You crashed about midnight, missed a lot of the action after that.'

Lionel started firing questions to us.

'You boomed it!' Lucky Phil yelled out. Lucky Phil then said, 'What about number six? "Who had the best boobs?" They were all fantastic,' he spurted out with his addictive laugh. We all cracked up laughing.

'What about number five?' Joe asked. '"Who made you feel special?"'

'What about number seven?' Lionel added. '"How many times did you ejaculate?" What's that?' said Lionel, then he suddenly said 'Lots,' and we all laughed so much, Lucky Phil unable to stop, he even got stomach cramps. We could not believe how something like this could happen to us. All I could think about was, were we set up? Were we conned?

I said to Lucky Phil, 'We all had a very good time last night, and this is the result of our experiences. Let's do the best we can to answer their questions.' Lucky Phil and Joe were still laughing.

Lionel said, 'I'm not happy answering some of these questions.' Joe and Lucky Phil started laughing hysterically.

As we all chuckled between ourselves over the answers we were giving, Simone came in.

'Boys,' she said, 'All done?' she spurted out as she collected the questionnaire from us all.

'We all have lots of questions for you,' Lucky Phil spurted out.

'No time for answers', Simone spurted out, as she gathers up the papers. 'The girls are waiting to go – we're late,' she explained. 'We must go now.'

'Go where?' Lucky Phil spurted out.

'Home,' said Simone.

'Let's go to the beach,' Lucky Phil spurted out.

'We must go now.' As she walked to the door, she asked, 'Got everything, boys? The rest of the girls are in the car park waiting for me, let's go.'

As we walked to the lifts, Lucky Phil was trying to get a contact phone number from someone, but she insisted no one wanted to be contacted by any of us.

'Look,' she spurted out, as Lucky Phil got louder in his questioning, 'We all had a great time, let's not spoil it now,' as the lift came to a halt in the car park. There was a silence as the door opened, and we saw the girls waiting in a four-wheel-drive. Flash looking machine, I thought, with them all squished in and loaded up with suitcases in the back and on a roof rack. All laughing, happy.

Simone went straight to the passenger's front door, already opened for her, I noticed. Lucky Phil ran around to Terry, who was driving, asking her to go to the beach.

Her instant response was, 'We're going home. Thanks for the orgy!' She yelled out to all of us.

'What's an orgy?' Lionel spurted out, as all the girls started chanting, 'Orgy! Orgy! Orgy! Boys! Boys! Boys!' as they drove away, echoing as they went up the ramp and away.

The look on Lucky Phil's face said it all. I thought he was going to shed a tear, something I had never thought I would see from Lucky Phil. As we all just stood there, dumbfounded by what we just heard, it finally sinks in. We have been sucked in, hook, line, sinker, so to speak.

This must have been the intention of Terry and Simone from when we all first met them. Lucky Phil was not conning them. They were conning him and us. Boy, was this a once in a lifetime experience for all of us.

As we slowly started walking back to our backpacker room, Lionel said he could not work it all out.

'They seemed such nice girls,' he said softly.

Joe spurted out, 'They were unbelievable'.

'I hope we meet them, again', Lucky Phil spurted out.

I was stunned by the whole night's experience.

Chapter 21

Fastest 24hrs – L.L.

Upon arriving back to the backpacker's pub, at about 10.30, the kind lady who booked us in the day before said, 'Are you boys coming or going?'

Joe spurted out, 'I can't come anymore,' with a fit of laughter from him and Lucky Phil. I whacked him behind the head.

'Calm down, Joe,' I spurted out. 'Sorry, lady, he's a bit tipsy.'

'Did you stay here last night?' she asked.

'No, but we paid to,' was my response.

'I thought you did not come back last night,' she said. 'Must have had a good night, boys.'

'The best,' was Lucky Phil's instant response.

'I think we're all going to have a sleep now,' Lionel added. 'Looks like you need it.'

As we walked to our room, Joe said, 'What's on?' to Lucky Phil. 'We have one more night here.'

'I'm going to bed,' he spurted out.

'Not all by yourself.' Joe killed himself laughing.

'Not funny, Joe,' Lucky Phil spurted out.

Lionel said that he also needed more sleep.

'You're kidding,' Joe spat out, 'You got more sleep than us.'

I said, 'A sleep sounds good to me.'

We all soon crashed in two beds. When I woke up, Joe was gone and Lionel and Phil were in deep discussion about the

events of last night. Lionel could not believe the details Lucky
Phil was telling him.

'Is it all true?'

'It's true, every bit of what I had heard Phil tell you.'

Then Joe walked in and spurted out, 'It's night time out
there. What's on?'

'How much money you got Joe?'

'Not much.'

'Don't look at me!' Lionel spurted out.

'Shit, I've got about 20 left. Art, what about you?'

'Well, thanks to Mum, and after paying for our room, I
now have enough to get some tea and enough for petrol to get
home tomorrow.'

'Looks like the beach tonight, boys,' Lucky Phil yelled out.
'Let's go. Being a Saturday night, it'll be very busy.'

'Lots of eye candy,' Joe said.

As we walk along the beach, all conversation was about
last night, the girls and that questionnaire. Lucky Phil said he
felt used by the girls and Joe spurted out, 'I want to be used
again,' and we all started laughing, except Lucky Phil, who
didn't seem to see the funny side of Joe's remark. Lionel said
this is the best holiday he has ever had, and wants to do it
again next year. We all agree.

'Let's check out the pub.'

'Might bump into Mandy or Teresa - or Bob!' Joe spurted
out, knowing this could spark Lucky Phil into a brighter
frame of mind.

'Good idea,' Phil spurted out. We all knew this was one
of Phil's favourite pastimes, chatting about girls in pubs. As
we all walked into the pub, straight away Phil spotted Bob,
surrounded by people. As Phil pushed through the crowd,
his loud voice called out, 'Bob! Boy, am I glad to see you!'

Bob also got excited to see Phil.

'Phil!' He yelled back. 'Everyone, this is Lucky Phil. A
good mate of mine,' he spurted out, as the rest of us just hung
back and got some beers.

Watching Phil and Bob, laughing and joking with Bob's friends, 'How does he do that?' Lionel asked.

Joe spurted out, 'It's his happy go lucky go friendly, and that laugh of his is addictive.'

We see Phil light up a smoke. 'Here we go,' said Joe, knowing that Bob's smokes are special. We all just sat back, watching and hearing Phil's laughter getting louder. Not long after this, Phil came up to us with this 'drop dead gorgeous' babe hanging on to his arm (about half his height, with Phil being tall, about six and a half feet, her being about four and a half feet).

Phil spurted out, 'We're off. Need to get 'something' from our room. Art give me our keys,' was his request. 'I'll be 'back soon',' he said with a wink. As they walked away, we all knew what that 'something' from our room was.

After about an hour they returned. 'Did you get 'lost'?' Joe spurted out. We all cracked up laughing.

Phil spurted out, 'Meet Bridget.'

'Hi boys,' she responded, as Phil introduced us to her.

'We decided to go for a walk around the beach, sorry we were gone so long,' she spurted out with a smile to Phil.

Phil went on to say that she lived in Toowoomba, here in Queensland. She was staying with her parents, and had not seen much of the Gold Coast. 'I'm going to show her around a bit. Catch you later,' Phil spurted out, as they walked off.

Not long after, Lionel asked, 'Did Phil give you back the keys?'

'No, he didn't.'

'Great,' said Lionel.

Joe asked Lionel what the time was.

'Shit, it's after midnight,' he spurted out.

'Let's go,' I said.

'What about Phil and the keys?' Lionel points out.

'Somewhere on the paper receipt I got, it said if you lose your key - ring a phone number, and they will open up for you. But I think it costs $10.'

'Phil can pay for this,' he spurted out.

After eventually getting into our room, about one hour later, as we were all in bed nearly asleep, Phil comes in, all smiles and happy as ever, and spurted out, 'I think I've just met my wife.'

We all jump up.

Joe says, 'Bridget the Midget.' Then we all burst out laughing,.

'Not funny,' Phil spurted out. 'She's very smart. We went back to her apartment, where she's staying with her parents.'

'Comes with parents,' Joe said as he cracked up again laughing (we all couldn't stop laughing). The thought of Phil-saying 'wife Bridget' and 'parents' was all too much for us.

I said to Phil, 'I never thought I would hear the word 'wife' from you.' Now we were all getting stomach cramps laughing.

Phil stormed out of the room, slamming the door. 'Shit,' said Joe with us all still laughing.

About 15 minutes later, Phil came back. 'Sorry Phil,' was all I could think of to say.

As he climbed into bed, Joe said to Phil that he had never seen him so 'serious' about a girl before.

'I know she's a 'bit' shorter than me. A 'bit',' spurted out Joe. 'But she is so interesting and smart. Her parents are fantastic and invited me to come and visit then whenever I want to. This has never happened to me before,' he spurted out.

'Are you sure this is not Bob's smokes doing this to you?' Joe spurted out.

'No' Phil spurted out.

Lionel then spurted out, 'Did you and Bridget get into it in here?'

'On your bed,' Phil spat out.

Lionel jumped off his bed. 'On here?'

Phil gave us a smile. 'She was absolutely incredible. We just click. Not just the sex, but we have so much in common.'

'You feeling OK?' Joe spurted out.

'I've got her address and phone number. We will see what happens,' was his response.

'What's the plan for tomorrow?' Phil spurted out.

Joe popped up, 'Art wants to leave about 'six or seven' – ('PM I hope,' says Phil).

'What, in about four to five hours?' Lionel spurted out.

'If I can sleep at all after this weekend,' I spurted out, all of us now laughing. All went to sleep.

Chapter 22

Back home to 'Bombshell' – N.F.M., L.L.

With me waking up first then waking the other boys, 'Let's go,' I piped out. 'We'll get brekkie on the road.'(Fuel up with food and petrol).

As we returned our keys to the nice lady on our way out of backpacker's pub, and got our small deposit box, she wished us, 'Good luck going home.' Everyone laughed.

As we took it in turns driving back to Melbourne, I said, 'It should be quicker going home – going downhill towards Melbourne,' I suggested (not everyone agrees with this).

In talking about the whole holiday experience, we decided not to tell 'anybody' about our last couple of days.

'Too embarrassing,' said Lucky Phil, (not feeling so Lucky at all, I think).

'He was happy to meet Bridget,' I spurted out, to help Phil brighten up a bit.

'Yep that's for sure,' he spurted out.

Things went a bit quiet for a while, then Lucky Phil said, 'I've been thinking about a song, just made up for our friends. Let's call it "Twin Lips",' he spurted out, I think to stir me up a bit. He started:

Twin lips,
Take my tips,
Which lips do you kiss,
Up high, down low,
How far will you go,

I know how it feels,
To be lost in deals,
How do you know how it feels,
For your lady,
How likes to do deals,
Up we go to find her,
Thinking of the past,
Only to find it does not last,
Home we go with some results,
What a trip you have had,
But with faults.
Would I do it again,
You bet without any regret.

Then that addictive laugh, with all of us now laughing.

Now approaching night time, flying alone, it was my turn to sleep. *Thank god,* I thought. It was Lionel's turn to drive (he is rapt again). I told Joe, 'Keep him awake.'

'I'm too excited,' Lionel spurted out, with Phil and I in the back seat, asleep, me dreaming of getting home, seeing family, thinking of Al and Kay.

I woke up. It was still dark, mid-morning. Joe was asleep, radio down low, Lionel softly singing to himself.

'How long has Joe been asleep for?' I spurted out.

'A couple of hours, I guess,' spurted out Lionel.

'How you feeling, Lionel?' I asked

'Okay,' he answered. I could tell he needed a break.

'Pull into the next town,' I spurted out. I could see lights on a hill coming up. This will do, as we pulled up outside a newsagents, milk bar, food store, the lot, I guess.

The man was only just opening up, so I asked if he is now open.

'Depending on what you want,' he said. 'Probably just drinks are all I can do now.'

'Good idea,' spurted out Lionel. 'Drinks to go then.'

As I took over driving, and the sun came up (beautiful sunrise I think, I love sunrises), slowly, the boys woke up.

'Where are we?' Phil questioned.

'Not far now to 'home',' I answered. 'Drinks there for you, boys.'

'Great, thanks,' Joe spurted out.

After dropping the boys to their homes, I was keen to tell Al and the girls, Mum and Dad, about some of our experiences. (Dare not tell all.) As we sat around the table, I told Al and my sisters about the beaches, high rise apartments, busy pubs, karaoke nights.

Mum couldn't get over how much money we spent.

'I will pay you back tomorrow. Going to the bank first thing in the morning, and put it into your bank account.'

'Thank God for that,' Mum said.

Al piped in and said, 'While you were away, a couple of things have changed.' Was he throwing a spanner in the works with his next comment? 'Kay and I are having twins – not one, but two babies,' he spurted out (another bombshell) – as he explained, 'It's been decided. Kay and I are going to live with Kay's Mum and Dad. There's more room in their house.'

Mum looked very sad, and said nothing. (Everyone looked sad I thought.)

Boy, did I miss him, in the bungalow. I never thought this would happen.

The twins are born, one boy, one girl, and everyone was so excited.

Chapter 23

Another Family – N.F.M., L.L.

Upon arrival of the twins, a whole new life began. Mum was always on Al's back to 'bring them to see her'. Mum just melted them into her arms, one on each arm, it was the best moment I can remember.

My little sisters could not get enough of them as well, trading them like 'dolls'. They loved pushing them around the house and outside, in the backyard, in their twin pram. The twins are spoiled by everybody. 'Truly loved' like we all were as children. Showing everything Dad had made for Mum, fish in ponds, chook shed, pigeons, budgies, even showing them off to our neighbours.

Oh, the sisters loved them both so much, like 'little mothers' – I think. At this time, I was working a lot, saving hard for a new car, my 'dream car'. I decided to buy a brand-new Holden, not a Sedan, but a panel van. Around this time, panel vans or Sandmans, as they are called, are starting to become popular with young people. For the flexibility as 'tradies' or 'pleasure' type vehicles.

With both these ideas in mind, 'trade for working', 'pleasure for camping' (no longer in tents), I ordered a one-off, 308 VB purple-coloured (the latest colour), panel van. My dream car. With its special colour, side windows, it would take a couple of weeks to deliver. I could not wait with excitement, at this point, and I told Al, who had just got his licence but didn't own a car, that he could have my old FB Sedan.

He was over the moon with this car. Now he had 'total freedom'. I told him about my experiences with speeding and reminded him of his responsibilities and to look after it. He was so excited, 'I'm telling Kay now,' he spurted out.

When I received my new car, boy, was it special. It needed mag wheels, a loudspeaker system, purple curtains on side, and a mattress in the back, for camping of course. All done within weeks. It looks perfect, I thought.

At this time, about to turn 20, I have my dream car, now I wanted a dream bike, a 250CC Yamaha dirt bike.

I bought a second-hand one I find for sale, almost same colour as my panel van, but it did not fit in the back of the panel van (oops), so I bought a second-hand trailer, big enough for four bikes; room for mates' bikes and camping gear. It was not a very flashy trailer, a bit old but cheap.

I soon fixed this by putting mag wheels on it (to suit my panel van) then sprayed it the same colour as my panel van, of course. I soon got the nickname 'Purple People Eater', with my purple panel van, purple trailer and purple bike. I felt on top of the world.

To top this off, I also dressed up in all purple clothes – including shoes – at a party I went to, dressed 'as above'. What a sight this must have been to some people! Everybody started laughing and joking. The purple clothes got the flick after that party.

Everything else lasts for a long time, with work, play, parties, friends: life is at its best. Now at 20, single, with lots of friends, male and female, I was very happy, still working hard, making good money, and wondering, 'What will happen next in my life?'

So up to this point of my life, I have opened up my heart and soul. Should I carry on with my life story? Or not. Is it too much to reveal to my entire family? Or not.

I hope all the information, experiences, so far, may answer some of these, and other questions, as to my growing up in a world full of surprises. Nothing surprises me anymore. Life will always have its ups and downs. I will try to overcome anything that challenges or confronts me.

With the help from all my family and friends, clients, I have survived so far, thank you all.

www.ingramcontent.com/pod-product-compliance
Lightning Source LLC
Chambersburg PA
CBHW060233030426
42335CB00014B/1427